STIAN WINTERS

THE AUTOBIOGRAPHY

RUSSIAN WINTERS
THE AUTOBIOGRAPHY

ANDREI KANCHELSKIS
IN COLLABORATION WITH TIM RICH

Best Wishes

deCoubertin
BOOKS

First published as a hardback by deCoubertin Books Ltd in 2017.

First reprint

deCoubertin Books, Studio I, Baltic Creative Campus, Liverpool, L1 OAH
www.decoubertin.co.uk

ISBN: 978-1-909245-49-5

A CIP catalogue record for this book is available from the British Library.

Cover design and typeset by Thomas Regan | Milkyone Creative.

Printed and bound by Jellyfish

'I don't think I could love you so much if you had nothing to complain of and nothing to regret. I don't like people who have never fallen or stumbled. Their virtue is lifeless and of little value. Life hasn't revealed its beauty to them.'

Boris Pasternak, Doctor Zhivago

This book is dedicated to my parents and my children, Andrei and Eva, and to my first coaches, Valery Karpinus and Nikolai Koltsov – and to the memory of George Scanlan.

Andrei Kanchelskis, Moscow, 2017.

CONTENTS

FOREWORD

RYAN GIGGS

THE FIRST THING ANY OF US AT MANCHESTER UNITED noticed about our new signing, Andrei Kanchelskis, back in 1991 was that he was so quick. There are some players whom we like to describe as deceptively quick. Perhaps they have a slower acceleration, a more languid running style, a longer stride. But there was nothing deceptive about Andrei's pace. He was quick-quick. He was bloody-hell quick.

The second thing we noticed, which might not have been so apparent outside of United, was that Andrei had an astonishingly powerful right-foot shot. I don't think that I had ever seen anyone hit the ball as hard as Andrei could. He was built perfectly for a footballer: lean on top with massive legs that generated all that power. He looked like a winger should look, leaning over the ball as he went forward, arms out for balance, favouring the long-sleeved version of those classic Adidas and Umbro strips we wore in the last days of the old First Division, and then the dawn of the Premier League.

When Andrei joined the club, I had made my debut earlier that month as a 17-year-old winger and while I was determined to tie down my own place in the team I also knew that the competition was going to be tough. We had Lee Sharpe, who was brilliant in the run to the 1991 European Cup-Winners' Cup final, and then there was Andrei, doing what all great wingers do: drawing the full-back in, putting the ball past him and hitting the accelerator.

It is safe to say that the first time I ever heard of a club called Shakhtar Donetsk was when I read about our new signing from the Soviet Union. Those were very different times when there was not the access to footage, statistics and informed opinion in English about the leagues around Europe and the wider world. Signing what we referred to then as a Russian footballer – although I know that Andrei was born in the Ukraine – was something new and exotic. Football is simple once the ball comes out and although conversation with Andrei was limited in those early days he was quickly one of the lads.

When I think of Andrei, I immediately think of his interpreter George. George Scanlan, I have later learned, was a professor of modern languages at what is now Liverpool John Moores University, who was also a non-league football manager himself. All I can say is that Sir Alex Ferguson must have trusted George completely because he was invited right into the inner sanctum of United. He was there in the team talks and he was also permitted to sit on the bench so he could give Andrei the instructions Sir Alex needed to pass on. Very few outsiders over the years were afforded that privilege.

Despite the language barrier, Andrei threw himself into life at United. He would come with us on nights out and although the conversation in those early days largely involved him listening and nodding, he always wanted to be part of the group. I did not give it much thought then but looking back it must have been difficult for Andrei to assimilate, coming from a country so different to Britain, which had been so isolated, but that never stopped him from being a good team-mate.

In those days the club did not have the infrastructure to look after foreign signings that it does now. Andrei had to get himself into training from his home in Cheshire and I recall a few times when he did get lost on the way. There might also have been a couple of occasions when Greater Manchester Police had to enlighten him as to the speed limit but he settled down quickly.

I am sure Andrei will not mind me saying that, in the loud and demanding dressing room we had at United in those days, his dress sense came under scrutiny from his team-mates. Andrei was obsessed with Versace. Versace shoes, Versace jeans, Versace shirt. Was he aware, we would often inquire, that other labels were available?

Andrei was a favourite with the United fans. A hat-trick at home against Manchester City in November 1994 guaranteed that. I remember his goal that year against Oldham in the FA Cup semi-final replay at Maine Road. In April 1993 we both scored in a 3-1 win at Carrow Road over a Norwich City team who were then credible title contenders. The pace and power of United on the counter-attack that day was something else.

I won't forget another he scored against Leeds at Old Trafford in a 2-0 win in September 1992 when I crossed from the right side with outside of my left foot and Andrei got his head on it at the back post. That goal was unusual because he was on the left and

I was on the right. We would occasionally take it upon ourselves to switch sides if we felt that we were not having the effect on the game that we wanted.

Looking back at the footage of those years reminds me what great times they were when United attacked teams with pace and confidence. A whole generation of United fans remember that era with such fondness. I know because I live in Manchester and people love to talk about those days.

Andrei left in that summer of 1995, and although with hindsight his departure and the exit of Paul Ince and Mark Hughes opened the door for Paul Scholes, David Beckham and Nicky Butt, it does get forgotten what a big call that was from Sir Alex. Andrei, Incey and Sparky were at the top of their game, or at least very close to it. They were major players in a team that had won two Premier League titles, including the double in 1994, and very few clubs would have been able to replace them.

I saw Andrei in Moscow before the 2008 Champions League final and it was great to catch up. It is the nature of old team-mates that our careers and our lives take us in different directions. One thing will never change, however, and that is the games we played together, the goals we scored and the trophies we won. If you were a United player in the 1990s then you were part of a golden era.

It is a pleasure for me to introduce Andrei's autobiography and I hope that reading it will stir United fans' memories of a time when it felt that our club was awakening, with a boldness that would see us conquer England and then Europe all over again. Andrei was a big part of it and at Old Trafford that will never be forgotten. I wish my old team-mate, and a fine United footballer, the very best.

Ryan Giggs, Manchester, May 2017

1
THE CENTRE OF THE WORLD

WHEN WE GATHERED ROUND THE TELEVISION, OUR nation felt like the centre of the world. It was the summer of 1980. I was eleven years old living in Kirovograd, a provincial city in what is now Ukraine. Far away in Moscow, they were staging the Olympic Games.

It is remembered for the duel between Sebastian Coe and Steve Ovett and for the boycott by the United States. Some of us can still remember the mascot, Misha, the bear. The athletics events were staged in what was then called the Lenin Stadium and is now the Luzhniki, where Manchester United won the Champions League and where the World Cup final will be held, 38 years after the Olympics.

I was growing up in the Soviet Union, one of the two superpowers that held the world in balance. It was at the height of the Cold War. The Soviet Union had invaded Afghanistan and Ronald Reagan was about to become president of the United States. Mikhail Gorbachev, who would change everything with his policies of *glasnost* (openness) and *perestroika* (reconstruction), had just been elected to the politburo but nobody really knew who he was. The president was Leonid Brezhnev, an old, hard-line Communist, who said nothing memorable, ever.

When I joined Manchester United in May 1991, the Soviet Union was on the point of collapse but there was still ignorance and suspicion about us. When I went to Manchester, people thought bears walked the streets of Moscow. 'Yeah,' I would reply. 'We shake their hands and say hello.'

In the summer of 2018, Russia will once more feel like the centre of the world. The Soviet Union has long gone and it has taken the old Communist order with it but there is still plenty of suspicion about Russia. Vladimir Putin is analysed and mistrusted in the same way as Brezhnev and Gorbachev were.

Putin is not a big football fan; his sport is ice hockey. However, he knows the value of putting on a show as he proved with the Winter Olympics in Sochi. They cost more than £5 billion and they practically built a new town there.

The World Cup will bring new stadia, new airports and, with them, jobs. St Petersburg will have what will be, until the World Cup comes to Qatar, the most expensive football stadium on the planet.

The story of the Krestovsky Stadium is almost the story of the last decade of Russian football. It was supposed to have opened in 2008, the year that Zenit St Petersburg beat Glasgow Rangers in Manchester to win the UEFA Cup.

But then came the financial crash. The main sponsor, Gazprom, pulled out. The architect, Kisho Kurokawa, died. Then came sanctions imposed because of the invasion of Crimea. It finally opened in April 2017 at a cost of more than £1 billion.

Those Manchester United fans who made the long journey to Rostov the month before the Krestovsky opened saw their team play in a little open bowl of a ground on a pitch that was unfit for football, where the ball spat, squatted and moved in all kinds of directions.

On the south bank of the River Don, a new stadium was nearing completion. It will seat 45,000 and a new hub of the city will be built around it. If Manchester United play Rostov again, their fans will find the ball bounces rather better and the view is rather more comfortable.

Moscow's new stadium, the Otkrytie, which is due to stage the first match of the World Cup, tells another story. It belongs to Spartak Moscow, the most famous and best-supported club in Russian football.

Spartak have been playing since they were founded by Nikolai Starostin in 1934 but this is the first time they have had their own ground. Before, they would play at the Luzhniki and, earlier still, they would share Lokomotiv's ground.

Unlike the other Moscow clubs, Dynamo, Torpedo and CSKA, what made Spartak so popular was that they had no direct connection with the state. Clubs called Dynamo were part-funded by the security services and Lavrenty Beria, who was Stalin's head of the secret police, supported Dynamo Moscow. Starostin was sent to the gulag. If you go to the Otkrytie, you will see a statue of Starostin and his brothers.

In 2017, Spartak Moscow won the Russian Premier League for the first time in sixteen years, managed by Massimo Carrera, who used to be Antonio Conte's assistant with Italy and at Juventus. In London and Moscow, Conte and Carrera won the title in the same week 1,500 miles apart, but perhaps Carrera's achievement was a bigger one.

How the world will see Russia depends on how the World Cup tournament is managed. There are a lot of nerves, plenty of excitement and a lot of pride. This is the first time a World Cup has ever been staged in eastern Europe.

Predicting football can be a foolish business. The bombing of the St Petersburg metro that killed fourteen in April 2017 is a warning of what can happen but the World Cup in Russia, just like those in South Africa and Brazil, should be safe. Or as safe as any state can make it.

The European Championships in France had very high levels of security and were very well organised but they could not prevent the rioting in Marseilles that disfigured England's opening game against Russia or the atrocity that followed the final on the Promenade des Anglais in Nice, where a truck was driven into a crowd.

I have been involved in meetings with the World Cup organisers to discuss how incidents like that can be stopped. My advice is that you must take every precaution but you cannot guarantee nothing will happen.

In the run-up to great sporting events, a lot of things are said to cover the backs of the people organising them. So the Athens Olympics would never be ready, everyone coming to South Africa 2010 would be shot, everyone coming to Brazil four years later would be robbed.

Information makes you stronger. Going to places is always better than watching from afar on television. The Russian World Cup will be the third in succession where people will hesitate before going. Before the tournaments in South Africa and Brazil, we were told that you risked being shot or at the very least mugged the moment you set foot outside your hotel.

I was thinking of going to the 2014 tournament but even the Brazilian footballers in Russia told me that it would probably be too dangerous. When you speak to those who did go to Rio de Janeiro, Fortaleza or Salvador, they will tell you only what a fabulous experience it was.

In Russia at least there is less suspicion of the West than there used to be. The Soviet Union was a closed society. People in the big cities, in Moscow and St Petersburg, have more of an idea of what is going on around them than my parents' generation would have done.

In 1989 I went with Dynamo Kiev to London to play in a pre-season tournament at Wembley. It was also about that time that I began travelling abroad with the Soviet Union's Under-21 sides.

We were told to be careful. People in the West might try to provoke or entrap us. We were told to be very wary of going shopping because we might, at any time, be accused of shoplifting. We were told to watch what we said and, if someone gave us a present, it would be best not to accept it. On no account were we to leave the hotel on our own.

Although there are many, many people who have never left Russia, that is one way in which the change has been for the better. People do travel, they do know much more about what lies beyond the borders. If you go to Russia, you will find people friendly, happy to talk football, especially about the Premier League, which attracts more viewers than Russian domestic football.

English is more widely understood than it was when I was growing up, when nobody saw the need to learn a foreign language.
Why would we? Most people would never leave the Soviet Union,
there would be no need to speak anything but Russian.

When Manchester United came to play Rostov, which has a very
passionate fan-base, the Rostov supporters gave them blankets as
a gift because even in southern Russia it can grow very cold on
a March night. The Manchester United team hotel was besieged
by fans hoping for a glimpse of the players. Rostov is famous for
its fish market and its caviar but it is also one of the places that
deserves a World Cup.

I always think it is a good idea to see things with your own eyes
and then talk. Too many people, especially in this age of the internet, talk and write about things they have little knowledge of.

That applies to football more than almost anything else. Sometimes, I will find myself in a hotel foyer or at an airport departure
lounge talking to a stranger and he will tell me he is good friends
with Sir Alex Ferguson. I will stop the conversation, hand them my
phone and say, 'Why don't you call him, I am sure he would love
to hear from you.'

I was surprised that Russia won the race to stage the World Cup
if only because football there was a sport that seemed to be on the
wane. The fear is that the team that represents Russia will not do
the tournament justice. When the Soviet Union fell apart, so, too,
did other things, and football was among them.

The Russian team is in such a sorry state that, if we were not
hosting the tournament, we probably would not have qualified for
it. Stanislav Cherchesov, the national manager, had been roundly

condemned even before the opening of the Confederations Cup, the now-traditional dry run for the World Cup. Friendlies have been lost to Costa Rica, Ivory Coast and Qatar.

If England's defeat to Iceland provided the most embarrassing exit from Euro 2016, then at least they qualified for the knockout stages. Russia finished last in England's group; their sole point came from the draw with England in Marseilles that will be remembered only for the crowd violence.

In 2008, Zenit St Petersburg won the UEFA Cup and Guus Hiddink took Russia to the semi-finals of the European Championship. In the decade that followed, Russian football has collapsed.

Part of the problem is the Russian Football Union has so few members who have played the game or managed a football team. Sometimes, when you speak to them, they seem to be talking a forgotten language.

For Russia, as for England, Euro 2016 was an embarrassment. They had both employed Fabio Capello when their fortunes had reached rock bottom. Capello qualified each country for a World Cup and then, in South Africa and Brazil, watched as those two nations disappeared without trace. In Brazil, Capello's Russia did not win a game, finishing third in their group behind Algeria.

The fact remains that, since the end of the Soviet Union, Russia has qualified for three World Cups, been knocked out in the group stages each time and won two matches from nine – against Cameroon and Tunisia.

Every football nation goes through a time of decline and it was Capello's misfortune to manage Russia at a time when football there was at such a low ebb. What kept being mentioned – and what people didn't forget – was that Capello was being paid £6m a year. That was double what Joachim Low earned for winning the World Cup with Germany.

A few months after Capello's team returned from Brazil, the Russian Football Union said they could no longer afford to pay him. Leonid Slutsky, who was manager of CSKA Moscow, took the team to France on the basis that he would not draw a salary. Like Capello in Brazil, he did not collect a win bonus.

They took that single point against England in Marseilles. It would not have mattered who was in charge – Capello or Slutsky – the results in Euro 2016 would have been the same.

When Slutsky qualified Russia for France by finishing above Sweden in qualification, there was a brief wave of euphoria about what we could achieve but, once the tournament began, the results were coldly, grimly predictable.

Cherchesov's target is to reach the World Cup semi-finals. Russia is a big country with a big population but there are very few who believe he is capable of anything approaching that. Whenever we are told that Russian football is progressing, the word 'progressing' always appears in quotation marks.

The one thing the last two World Cups had in common was that the hosts exited the competition embarrassingly. South Africa became the first host nation to be eliminated in the group stage. Brazil did make the semi-finals but were thrashed 7–1 by Germany. The fear is that Russia may build great stadia but the national team will be unworthy of them.

One thing the World Cup will do – and one thing that Russia desperately needs – is that it will encourage young people to get out of their bedrooms, put away their PlayStations and their phones and play football.

At least it is being held where a World Cup should be held, in a large country where fans can experience the differences of a nation. The tournament will be played out on a vast landscape. There will be games in Kaliningrad, an isolated city on the Baltic (which, before the Second World War, used to be Konigsberg in Germany). They will play in St Petersburg, in Samara, in Volgograd, in Rostov, Nizhny Novgorod and elsewhere.

If you come to follow your team you will see the 'white nights' of St Petersburg, where it truly never grows dark over the palaces and golden domes of the city. If you are in Rostov you can cruise on a boat down the River Don, once the great artery of the Cossack nation, and picnic on an island.

You can go to Volgograd and see where in 1943, when it was called Stalingrad, the tide of history changed. You will discover Russian beer is very cheap and not very good – you're better off buying imported German lager rather than Baltika, the biggest brand of Russian beer, brewed in St Petersburg.

The games will attract crowds, although I wouldn't put too much store by statements that a stadium is sold out. When Moscow staged the 2008 Champions League final between Chelsea and Manchester United, everyone was told there was no chance of getting a ticket. But when you actually got inside the Luzhniki Stadium on that rainswept night in May, you saw swathes of empty seats.

It will be the empty seats when the World Cup is done that might be the real problem for Russia. When I began playing for Dynamo Kiev in the late 1980s, the game against Spartak Moscow would attract 100,000 fans. There are nothing like those kinds of attendances in the Russian Premier League.

Spartak, the best-supported club in the country, get about 30,000. Zenit St Petersburg attract about 20,000. How will Zenit fill the world's most expensive football stadium? And how many empty seats will there be in the stadia at Ekaterinburg, Volgograd and Kaliningrad once the tournament has packed up and gone away and Russia no longer finds itself the centre of the world?

2
A SOVIET KIND OF GUY

I WAS IN MOSCOW, ABOUT TO RECEIVE AN AWARD for something or other from a Russian author and comedian called Mikhail Zadornov. He turned to me and said, 'You have a Lithuanian surname, your mother was from Ukraine, you grew up in the Soviet Union and you played for Russia. Who exactly am I giving this award to. Who are you?'

I have a British passport and, unlike almost everyone else in Russia, I drink tea with milk. But at heart I suppose I am a Soviet kind of guy. When somebody says to me, 'I am from Russia,' or 'I am from Ukraine,' something inside me stops.

When I was growing up it was all one country, the largest in the world that stretched over eleven time zones. I had friends from Armenia, from Azerbaijan, from Georgia. My mother still lives in the city where I was born. It was called Kirovograd then. It is not called Kirovograd any more.

When Ukraine became independent, the name Kirovograd was thought to be too Russian. It had been named after Sergei Kirov, who ran Leningrad in the 1930s until he was assassinated, probably on Stalin's orders. The name of Leningrad was also changed. It was thought to be too Communist. My mother, Yevgenia, now lives in Kropyvnytski. She hasn't moved.

My sister has. In 1992, the year after I joined Manchester United, Natasha met a Jewish man and went with him to Eshkol in southern Israel.

It was a good time for both of us to be getting out. They called it 'The Evil Nineties'. The Soviet Union had fallen apart completely. Our country, or what we thought was our country, had defaulted on its national debt repayments. The economy went through the floor.

The Soviet Union had gone but, in Kirovograd, the queues for food still remained. Now there was racketeering and violence. You'd go out on to the street and you could hear gunfire. Everyone seemed to have a pistol and be in a gang. The legal system had collapsed, nobody could get hold of the police so, if you had an issue, you sorted it out yourself.

I was 21 years old, playing for Shakhtar in the coal-mining city of Donetsk, when the Soviet Union began to disintegrate. I had a friend in Donetsk who was a boxer and because of that he got work with the mafia as 'security'. Wrestlers were also much in demand with the mafia. Because of my friendship with him I felt reasonably safe in the city, but others were not so lucky. If you were a businessman, you were suddenly very vulnerable.

Under the Soviet system, they allocated you an apartment depending on how many people you had to accommodate. You would be given so many square feet per person and you could wait up to twenty years for a flat.

Shakhtar had given me a car, a Volga. In the Soviet Union, if you drove or were driven in a Volga, it was a sign you had made it. Yuri Gagarin's reward for being the first man in space was a Volga. I decided to sell mine. A Georgian guy offered me 100,000 roubles for it, which was a fortune. It had cost 16,000. There was money everywhere. There was just nothing to spend it on.

The bloke who bought my car knew what he was doing. When there was a second debt default in 1992, the currency became increasingly worthless. People who had savings accounts lost almost everything.

Those who worked in banks or in government had got wind of the coming devaluation and could convert roubles to dollars. If the bank thought you were a 'good customer', the manager might take you to one side and say, 'A crash is coming. Maybe you should go out and buy something big.'

It was the time of the oligarchs, men like Roman Abramovich, Boris Berezovsky and Mikhail Khodorkovsky. Some of them took out what seemed like huge loans to buy sectors of the old Soviet economy; when the time came to pay those loans back, the currency had been devalued so much they owed very little but owned a lot.

In the Soviet Union sportsmen were not well paid by Western standards but they had a certain status. You would be treated as if you were a doctor. The footballers I knew when I left for Manchester still received their salaries, whereas many didn't. The mafia then would leave them alone. Now, they rob anybody.

Recently, I turned on the television in Moscow and heard that some celebrities had been robbed or burgled. That would never have happened in the 'Evil Nineties'. The godfathers in the mafia would have looked after them. No money would change hands but there would be an unwritten understanding that they would not be touched. Their fame would protect them. Now there are no rules.

My father, Antanas, was a lorry driver. He did not live to see the disintegration of the Soviet Union, although he should have done. He was just 42 when he died in 1986. Antanas was the middle of three brothers and the others lived to be 41 and 43.

Dad was a heavy smoker, like all his family. I can remember being taken into the pubs and the air would be thick with tobacco smoke. On the counter there would be a couple of bowls of salted fish. Dad would order a beer; I would have the fish, which was laid out for the same reason that pubs in Britain have bowls of peanuts. The salt makes you want to drink more.

Once, some friends and I stole sweets and cigarettes from a kiosk but when I came back, reeking of tobacco, my mother flew into a rage and threatened to tell my father. I stopped there and then.

In the Soviet Union they did not pay a pension but would put a certain percentage of your salary in a savings book. If you earned 120 roubles a month, then ten would go into your savings account. But Dad was 42; he had been working for only twenty years so there wasn't much in his savings book. And once we had paid for the cost of the funeral, there wasn't much left to keep us going. When the currency was devalued what was in the savings book became less and less.

My father's family had once been reasonably wealthy farmers in Lithuania. Between the wars the Baltic states were independent and Lithuania flourished. However, in August 1939, Molotov and

Von Ribbentrop signed the Nazi–Soviet Non-Aggression Pact. It astonished the world and sealed the fate of my father's family.

In return for giving Germany a free hand in the west to attack France, Stalin was given an undertaking that Hitler would tolerate his invasion of the Baltic states. In June 1940 the Red Army rolled into Lithuania and for my grandparents that meant one thing. They were considered to be rich peasants or in Russian, a *kulak*.

In Ukraine, where my mother's parents were living, to be considered a *kulak* was a death sentence. The 1930s had seen millions driven from their farms to either be shot or sent to Siberia. Their land was turned into collective farms and the famine that this caused saw millions perish. In Ukraine it is compared to the Holocaust and called the *Holomodor*.

In Lithuania, my grandparents thought it was preferable to slaughter their animals rather than give them up to the collective farms and that created a deep, lasting hurt. People like them learned to hate the Soviet Union and that hate was passed on to their children. When the Soviet Union collapsed, they turned their hate on to Russia because to them Russia was the Soviet Union in new clothes.

When my father told them he was going to marry my mother, Yevgenia, they disapproved to the extent that only one member of his family – a cousin – came to the wedding. It was only when I started playing for Manchester United that the rest of my father's family got in touch. I think they believed there might be some money coming their way.

Yevgenia was from Kirovograd and Kirovograd was in Ukraine and in the 1960s, under the rigid rule of Leonid Brezhnev, Ukraine was considered an integral part of the evil empire. Seen from Lithuania, they were collaborators.

Antanas and Yevgenia had met at a dance in Kirovograd, where my father was doing his three years of military service. It was 700 miles from Kaunas 'Lithuania's second city, and it was 700 miles for a reason.

In the Soviet Union you never did your military service anywhere near where you lived. If there was an uprising, they wanted the soldiers to have nothing in common with those who were rebelling. Very soon, my father and mother had quite a lot in common.

I was born in 1969, after Stalin but before Gorbachev, the years when the Soviet Union seemed set in stone. Even though I grew up deep in Ukraine, we spoke Russian not Ukrainian.

In recent years, since the split between Russia and Ukraine, everybody seems to have to speak Ukrainian in public just so they can prove their 'patriotism'. Julia Tymoshenko, who led the Orange Revolution that saw Ukraine break their alliance with Russia, speaks Russian at home but slips into Ukrainian whenever the television cameras are turned on.

Among older people there is nostalgia for the Soviet Union and that is particularly true whenever you talk football. The Soviet Union was one of the powers of the game. They finished fourth in the 1966 World Cup; they won the European Championship in 1960 and reached the final three more times. Their most recent final was in 1988, just a year before the Berlin Wall came down.

No Soviet team has ever lifted the European Cup but Dynamo Kiev won the Cup Winners' Cup twice while Dynamo Tbilisi won it in 1981. Neither is part of Russia, which tells you a lot about how much Russian football has suffered after the collapse. The only Russian team to make a European final before the break-up were Dynamo Moscow, who lost the 1972 Cup Winners' Cup final to Glasgow Rangers, a team I was to play for. The loss of the Ukrainian teams and players was to cripple the Russian national team.

After the split CSKA Moscow beat Sporting Lisbon on their own ground, the Jose Alvalade, to win the UEFA Cup in 2005. Three years later, in Manchester, Zenit St Petersburg beat Rangers to lift the same trophy. For a decade there has been nothing.

If you were growing up in Kirovograd in the 1980s, you would be trained for employment in the big factories. The Red Star, where my mother worked, produced tractors and combine harvesters. Another built radios while a third manufactured parts for guided missiles and would always have officials walking around with Geiger counters to check radiation levels.

Chernobyl lay three hours' drive north of Kirovograd and in April 1986, when I was seventeen, the Geiger counters began going off the scale. Fortunately for my family, the radioactive cloud from the explosion that ripped the roof off the nuclear power station drifted northwards.

For about ten days nobody was told what had happened. Some officials in the local Communist Party were tipped off but they either chose not to say anything or they slipped away to Moscow.

Then gradually, by word of mouth, ordinary people like my family discovered what was happening at Chernobyl. There had been a call for builders to fly in and do 'construction work', but in reality they were dealing with the fires and its aftermath.

Even those who were trying to contain the explosion were not told what the dangers were. As the years went by, you heard of people dying early from strange causes.

By the time of Chernobyl, I had left Kirovograd to be part of a football academy in Kharkov, 230 miles to the east. Football was not my first love. My dream was to become an ice-hockey star. My hero was Valery Kharlamov.

He was small and dark – his mother was Spanish – and he scored brilliant goals for CSKA Moscow. They offered him a lot of money to go to Canada and play in the National Hockey League but Kharlamov was too much of a patriot to leave.

He led the Soviet team to two gold medals in successive Winter Olympics. He was also part of the Soviet side that lost to a United States college team in the 1980 Winter Olympics in Lake Placid, that in America they called 'The Miracle on Ice'.

The following year, his car, driven by his wife, hit a truck. The collision killed them both. CSKA retired Kharlamov's number 17 jersey until his orphaned son, Alexander, was old enough to wear it. When I joined Everton, I was told I could choose my squad number. Naturally, I picked 17, and when I was transferred to Fiorentina, I wore 17 for the same reason.

At school, the sport I specialised in was gymnastics, especially the rings and the bar, until one day a teacher suggested I should take up football. I fell in love with Diego Maradona.

I was seventeen when he took Argentina to the 1986 World Cup. I was already a professional footballer when Argentina met the Soviet Union in the 1990 World Cup in Naples, the city where Maradona played, where he was worshipped.

It was the second group game and, since both teams had lost their opening match, whoever lost would be in trouble. The game was goalless when Maradona handled the ball on the line. The referee gave nothing. Argentina won 2–0, the Soviet Union was eliminated in the group stage and Argentina went on to reach the final.

World Cups and major international tournaments were very big in the Soviet Union because there was usually very little football on television. If there was a televised sport that was on all the time, it was ice hockey.

The screening of football matches in the Soviet Union was very basic. There would be absolutely no build-up and no full-time analysis. The broadcast would begin when the referee blew his whistle to start the match and it finished when he blew for full time. Until the end of the 1980s, you watched in black-and-white.

Nobody even considered whether there might be coverage of foreign football. When I was growing up, Liverpool were the dominant team in Europe. Between 1977 and 1985 they were involved in five European Cup finals but I didn't see any of them and when I went to play in England I knew very little about Liverpool and even less about the other teams.

If you wanted to follow football, you tended to have to buy a newspaper and mine was *Gazeta Futbol-Khokkei*, half of which was devoted to football and half to ice hockey. They were the paper's only subjects. To me, it seemed a perfect combination. The coverage of sport in the main Soviet press was very formal. The back page of *Pravda* would have short, factual reports on the main football, hockey or athletics results without any comment.

Between them, my parents earned 250 roubles a month. In today's exchange rate, our monthly household income would be £3.50. However, in the Soviet Union, 250 roubles went a long way. I grew up in a three-bedroom flat and we seldom went short of anything.

Your household necessities – rent, telephone, gas, central heating – would probably be only thirty roubles. A suit cost sixty roubles, a Raketa watch, the kind supplied to the Red Army, cost 22. Food prices were controlled centrally by the government. Food was cheap; the trouble was that so much food was often unavailable.

We played outside, always. The Soviet Union had four television channels and none of them gave you much of an incentive to turn them on.

Kirovograd did have three cinemas, one of them named after Felix Dzerzhinsky, the founder of the KGB. The cinemas were open from nine in the morning to eleven at night and it cost ten kopecks (there are a hundred kopecks in a rouble) to get in.

People were fitter then. Facebook, mobile phones, PlayStations; they were yet to come.

In the Soviet Union, schools had numbers not names, a tradition that is still true of Russia today. I went to School 32. There were too many pupils and not enough schools, so you studied in shifts.

The first shift was from eight in the morning until one o'clock and the second shift from one until five. One week you did the morning shift and in the next week you would go in the afternoons. I did study English, although I made absolutely no effort. I did not see the point and could envisage no circumstances in which I would need to speak it.

We had to learn the poetry of Pushkin and Lermontov off by heart and recite it to the class. I liked the stories of Nikolai Gogol, like *The Overcoat* about an impoverished clerk who saves up to buy a coat. When he puts it on, his personality changes.

The only subjects I really enjoyed though were PE and what was called *Trud*. It means 'work' in Russian and involved learning carpentry or going around the school, cleaning, polishing or picking up litter.

Growing up, you went through various organisations. When you were eight years old you joined the Little Octobrists and at eleven you became a Young Pioneer. The Little Octobrists had a badge with a picture of Lenin; the Young Pioneers wore a red neckerchief. It was a bit like the cubs and scouts.

In the long holidays you would go to summer camp, often in the Crimea, where you would play tennis and football, go to dances or for walks in the forest. We would stroll through Gagarin Park in Yalta or go on a bus trip through the vineyards and tobacco farms to the Livadia Palace, where in 1945 Stalin, Roosevelt and Churchill settled the fate of post-war Europe.

As for family holidays, we went camping or rented an apartment by the sea. Hotels were out because they were invariably full and expensive. A car was out of our reach and out of most people's reach. If you had one, it marked you out. Having a car – a Lada or a Moskvitch – was something special.

When you were fifteen, you would apply to join the Young Communist League or Komsomol. If you wanted to go into further education, Komsomol membership was essential and you had to take a written test. Typical questions would be: 'When was the Communist Party of the Soviet Union founded?' Or: 'When was Lenin born?' There were a lot of dates and not everybody passed.

Like every town in the Soviet Union, Kirovograd had an organisation called the Society for the Olympic Reserve. It was dedicated to scouring schools for potential athletes, especially those who could go on to represent the country in the Olympics. When I was eleven, the Olympics were very big indeed. They were being staged in Moscow.

One day, School 32 had a visitor. His name was Valery Karpinus and he was from the Society for the Olympic Reserve. He wanted to watch a PE session and then he divided the group into two teams for a game of football. Afterwards, Karpinus asked three of us to remain behind.

He wanted us to join his football school, combining it with lessons at School 32. Gradually, I spent more time at the football school than the real thing. My sister, Natasha, became very good at writing letters explaining my absences. The emphasis of Karpinus's training was the importance of passing a football, how a single pass could take out an entire defence. Holding on to the ball too long was a sign of greed that could destroy a team. They were principles that carried me through my football career.

The training sessions were intense. If I was on the morning shift at school, I would go to the afternoon shift at Karpinus's academy and vice versa.

When I was fourteen, I came across another man who was to propel me on my way to becoming a footballer. He was Nikolai Koltsov. He had been a defender for Dynamo Kiev and he ran a sports' boarding school in Kharkov. It was 240 miles away. It specialised in athletics, gymnastics, swimming . . . and football.

My mum did not want me to go and neither did Karpinus, who thought I should wait another year and go to Kiev to train as a footballer when I was fifteen, but, eventually, Dad and I won the argument. He would have liked to have driven me there in his lorry, but instead we found ourselves waiting for the bus and the ten-hour journey to Kharkov.

More than a hundred others had made the same journey and waiting for us was a regime of sprints, ball-work and five-a-sides. Over three weeks in the summer of 1983, the hundred were whittled down to twenty.

Koltsov was a hard taskmaster. He had the kind of job that required you to be tough. He ran an almost military regime that had no concept of free time. We would get up at seven. Then we would train, have breakfast and go to school. In the evening there would be more training and on Saturday we would play a match.

There were classes every day. You studied the usual school subjects: Russian, geography, mathematics. I preferred history because Russia has such a very big history.

The history I learned was that of the Soviet Union: Lenin, the Revolution, the fall of the Romanovs and the storming of the Winter Palace. Mikhail Gorbachev had not yet taken power in Moscow; it was the last years of the old guard, Andropov and Chernenko. There was as yet no *glasnost*. It was all very traditional.

Your final grades were marked out of five. At most schools I would have got a five for sport but Koltsov gave me a four and a lecture about 'more work to be done'. There were academic lessons mixed in and, if you did badly in those, Koltsov had a remedy – a thirty-metre sprint repeated thirty times.

For Nikolai Koltsov there was always more work to be done. He was never satisfied but he did instil in me a burning desire to play for Dynamo Kiev. There is a Russian phrase that you 'become sick from wanting something' and I was becoming sick from wanting to play for Dynamo Kiev.

Then, one day in late January or early February, three of us were told to travel down to Sochi, 700 miles away on the Black Sea coast, where the local team, Metalist Kharkov, were undergoing the long pre-season training that in Russia they call *sbori*. When we arrived, the trainer studied me up and down and said, 'No use to me. Too small.'

I was the shortest in the academy and was playing as a number ten, modelling myself on the great Brazilian, Jairzinho. I told the trainer that if he stuck with me, I could be his Jairzinho. 'No chance,' came the reply. 'You are not tall enough for a start and I doubt you have the speed or the stamina.' Metalist said they would phone if they needed me. They never did.

Suddenly, I became very keen to become tall. I would stretch myself by hanging from a crossbar with someone holding my legs. I was told that carrots could increase your height, so naturally I stuffed myself with carrots and vitamins – anything to help me grow.

Not only was I one of the smallest at the academy, I was also the slowest. That might come as a surprise to anyone who watched me on the wing at Old Trafford but I had never done athletics.

I was told I had to improve my jumping so in the evenings, when nobody was looking, I would sneak out into a forest by the training pitches and practise jumping up and down on one leg, bringing my knee up to my chest. It was an exercise they called in Russian *Blokha* or 'the Flea'.

I would do it a hundred times and then I would swap legs and do it a hundred more. I would do it every evening for three years. I had dreams, like every teenage boy, and I could not imagine my life without football. I told myself that, if I had to train like this every day to become a professional footballer, that is what I would have to do. That was the price.

9
HOW TO STRIP A KALASHNIKOV

GRADUALLY, THE DREAMS BECAME BIGGER. THE first was to play for Kirovograd. Then I wanted to play for Dynamo Kiev and then for the Soviet Union. However, when I came back to Kirovograd, it was to a very different family.

Dad had died of a heart attack and money had become a problem. I had a go at a club called Zvezda, who would pay me and my mate, Igor Makagon, who had also gone to the Kharkov academy with me, eighty roubles a month each. It was half my dad's wage and it helped.

It was not just football that was on the horizon. The Soviet Union had two years of compulsory military service. Modern Russia still has military service but it is one year rather than two and you are exempt if you are a university student or have two children before you are twenty.

In the Soviet Union, one way of getting out of military service was to play for one of the army teams, like CSKA Moscow, or to play for clubs who were linked to the KGB. Those teams had Dynamo as a prefix. Dynamo Moscow and Dynamo Tbilisi all had historic links to the security police.

As the time to join the Red Army grew closer, I heard that Dynamo Kiev were interested in taking me on. In 1988, they were one of the most powerful teams in Soviet football, managed by Valery Lobanovsky, their greatest coach.

Lobanovsky was 49 when I arrived in Kiev. He had played for Dynamo as a winger and became their manager in 1973. He was a trained engineer and was interested in applying science to football. Lobanovsky somehow managed to get hold of a computer, which were very rare in the Soviet Union.

He took advice from Valentin Petrovsky, who had coached Valery Borzov to gold medals at the Munich Olympics, and within two years Dynamo had won the Cup Winners' Cup.

They had won it again in 1986, thrashing Atletico Madrid 3–0 in the final. They had players like Sergei Baltacha, Vasyl Rats, Igor Belanov, who was voted European Footballer of the Year, and Oleg Blokhin, who had played in the 1975 final.

Perhaps the player who summed Kiev up the most was Vladimir Bessonov. He was a centre-half but he could play as a full-back, as a midfielder, even at times as a striker. He won the Soviet league title in 1977 when he was nineteen and was still part of the side when they won the championship in 1990. He was absolutely fearless. He, Baltacha and I had the same coach when we were young, Nikolai Koltsov.

Dynamo Kiev were a wonderful side and Lobanovsky then shared the job of managing Kiev with being the manager of the USSR national side. Marcello Lippi and Fabio Capello used to come to Kiev from Italy to watch his training methods.

The summer I joined Dynamo he had taken the USSR to the European Championship final, where they had lost to a great Dutch side – Rijkaard, Gullit, Van Basten and Koeman. After the Soviet Union broke up, Lobanovsky left to work in the Arabian Gulf but he came back to Kiev late in his career and forged another great Dynamo Kiev side, the one featuring Andriy Shevchenko and Sergei Rebrov which lost to Bayern Munich in the 1999 Champions League semi-final. The calibre of the club I was joining and its manager was immense. The players were stars.

The contract with Dynamo Kiev meant I served only three months rather than two years military service but it was a dangerous time to be joining the Red Army. Far to the south there was a conflict between Armenia and Azerbaijan over a piece of territory called Nagorno-Karabakh.

Cracks had started to appear in the Soviet Union. We didn't grasp it but it was starting to fall apart. Nagorno-Karabakh was in Azerbaijan but the majority of people who lived there were Armenian. They demanded independence and soon the shooting started. We were told that when we finished our training we would be posted to Nagorno-Karabakh. Perhaps avoiding that war was the turning point of my life.

I had my invitation from Dynamo Kiev but the only way to use it was to catch the eye of a general or a senior officer and get him to sign my release papers. First, you had to arrange a meeting – and the conflict meant the person you wanted to see always seemed to have been sent to Moscow for consultations. Then, they had to be in a good enough mood to sign the piece of paper.

It was a tough three months. You would be up at six in the morning, then there would be training and shooting – although not the kind of shooting I had been used to at the Kharkov football academy. A lot of time was spent learning how to dig a foxhole. As the months went by, I thought I would never play football again. This was my life now.

I liked the discipline and, when I became a professional footballer, it served me well. As a teenager, I felt I was serving with honour. I was never tempted to buy the special certificates on the black market where a doctor had signed a form saying you were exempt because of illness.

I learned to love the Kalashnikov and had known how to fire one before I joined up. At school we had something called National War Preparation classes. We were taught how to strip down a Kalashnikov, clean the parts and put it back together.

The Kalashnikov is a fantastic rifle. One of the reasons it is so popular with guerrilla movements is that it is incredibly resilient. You can drop it in water, you can get sand in the mechanism and it will still fire.

Then, out of nowhere, I was told to travel to Kiev and report to Dynamo's academy. I was shown a communal living area. There was a canteen. I would be paid 250 roubles a month, about a quarter of the wages of one of the stars of the Dynamo side.

Back then, the Soviet leagues played from March to the end of November, which is logical in a country where temperatures can fall to minus-twenty or below in December and January.

In the close season there were the training camps – the *sbori*. In Russia there would be snow on the ground from the beginning of

December to the end of March. As a footballer, you can't just stop for three months. You had to keep training. You would go south: to Sochi, the Crimea or Georgia, anywhere where the temperatures were above freezing.

After the break-up of the Soviet Union, when travel became easier, teams would go to Spain, Turkey or elsewhere in the Mediterranean.

The first month of a *sbori* is always hard. You would begin in January after the New Year celebrations and everything would be geared towards physical fitness. You and your team are cooped up together in a training centre and worked constantly.

The second month is more enjoyable because you concentrate more on ball work and play friendlies. There are videos and tactical talks.

My mother never came to Kiev to watch me play. I suppose I was on the fringes of the Dynamo side and it wasn't certain that, if she came, I would be playing. She preferred to follow my progress in the newspapers or on television.

Plenty of people did come to the Olympic Stadium in Kiev where Dynamo staged their big games. Sometimes, there would be 100,000 there, more usually 60,000. It was not surprising. The passion for the game was enormous, the tickets were cheap, Kiev was a city of 2½ million and Dynamo was its only major club.

The big derby was against Spartak Moscow because this was a meeting between the Soviet Union's two most successful sides. The rivalry had become especially fierce since November 1976 when Dynamo had beaten Spartak 3–1 to relegate them from the Soviet Top League.

The atmosphere in a Dynamo–Spartak derby was always unforgettable. The nearest game I came across that had the same mixture of passion and hate was the one between Rangers and Celtic. You had to win. There was no alternative.

The derby did not survive the break-up of the Soviet Union. The last one in the league was a 3–2 win for Spartak in Kiev in 1991. Twenty-three years later, Dynamo Kiev were invited to open Spartak's new stadium, the Otkrytie. But this was the time of Russia's takeover of the Crimea and, although it was a friendly, it would be treated as far more than just a game of football. Dynamo refused to play.

In character and stature, there was something of Alex Ferguson in Lobanovsky, or should I say there was something of Lobanovsky in Ferguson. They possessed the same aura and, fortunately for my career, they both believed in wingers and a 4–4–2 system. Their style of play was remarkably similar, which is why my first full season at Old Trafford was so successful. I had very few adjustments to make save for the fact that the first and last matches in the Soviet Top League were played on artificial grass because of the weather.

There were differences. Sometimes, at Manchester United, Ferguson would charge into the dressing room, sweep stuff off any nearby table and begin shouting right into our faces.

Lobanovsky didn't shout. He just gave you a look, a stare and that would be enough. If you'd had a bad game, you tried not to catch his eye. If you did, it could be terrifying. He never raised his voice because he didn't have to and he did not believe in displaying his emotions in the same way Ferguson did.

You wouldn't have a one-to-one meeting with Lobanovsky in the way you would with Ferguson at Manchester United. The meetings would always be with the squad.

There was one time I did go to his office. Dynamo Kiev had

such a strong squad that even though I had broken into the Soviet Under-21 side, I was getting very few games. I was, however, attracting interest from Shakhtar Donetsk. I was told to go and see Lobanovsky, who was with Shakhtar's manager, Valery Yaremchenko, discussing my transfer. When Lobanovsky stared at you, it seemed he was looking right through you and when I left his office my shirt was soaked with my own sweat. He had accused me of betraying him without having said a word.

Not long before, Kiev had sold one of their greatest players, Aleksandr Zavarov, to Juventus and as part of the deal Dynamo had been presented with one of Juventus's team buses. It was a beautiful machine, with leather reclining seats and all kinds of little luxuries tucked away in the interior. We were used to buses made by Lada. One of the trainers came up to me and said, 'Do you want to go to Donetsk and rattle around in a Lada or do you want to stay here and be driven around in a Mercedes?' I wanted first-team football. I chose the Lada.

Zavarov was one of the first Soviet footballers to go abroad. A year later, in 1989, Sergei Baltacha left Kiev for Ipswich. Baltacha was a sweeper, who had been a product of the same Kharkov academy as I had, though he had graduated many years before.

He was thirty then and I don't think he went for the money. Ipswich were in the Second Division when he arrived and the salary would have been nothing like what Zavarov was being paid at Juventus.

When he left Kiev he told me he was unsure how his kids, Sergei, who was nine, and five-year-old Elena would settle in a new country. The Baltachas are still there, although Elena, who shone as a tennis professional, died tragically early from cancer.

However, once the Soviet Union started to break up, footballers became very keen to leave. Abroad seemed to guarantee stability, money and, more importantly, a future – things that suddenly seemed in very short supply in what was left of the old Soviet Union.

I may have been giving up a luxury team bus but moving east to Donetsk gave me other things. At Dynamo I'd been living in shared accommodation but Shakhtar gave me a two-roomed apartment, a Volga car and a salary of 700 roubles a month, which was nearly three times what I'd been earning in Kiev.

If you didn't make it in Kiev, Donetsk was a natural place to go. They took a lot of footballers from Dynamo and Yaremchenko told me that I would be one of his leading players.

Donetsk was a city built on coal. It was the centre of a vast mining region called the Donbass and for the miners football was their passion, their release from the pits. They lived for football, it brought them alive.

We played in a big bowl of a stadium that was in Donetsk's central park. The club left it in 2009 for the Donbass Arena, which staged the semi-finals of Euro 2012. Then, when civil war broke out in Ukraine, it came under artillery fire. Shakhtar abandoned it and took the club west, establishing their training ground and offices in Kiev and playing their home games in L'viv, 800 miles away near the Polish border.

After I joined we were taken to the mines to see how our supporters worked. It was not a journey for the faint-hearted. The conditions were terrible. The tunnels and the ledges were tiny; you had to crawl down them. The miners showed us how to drill the coal out of the seam. They had a canary with them to check for gas and I couldn't understand why these tough, hard men all wore eyeliner. There were so many particles of coal in the air that it coated their faces and they needed the make-up to keep their eyes clear of the grit.

It was a tremendously sobering experience to see how the men who stood on Shakhtar's terraces made their living. When we got above ground all of us were grateful we were footballers. The alternatives were the mines and the factories.

Miners in the Soviet system were very well paid because everyone knew they were risking their lives day in and day out. A footballer would earn the same as a miner but we would have additional privileges. We were allowed abroad to play in matches, for instance, and we would be given the sort of car you would have to wait years for. You might get a better apartment or a washing machine.

In the Soviet Union you didn't choose a career, you were directed or steered towards one. It was suggested to you that you should become a doctor, a miner, a footballer or a factory worker. The really high pay and privileges went to university professors, civil servants, the men in the government. Then came the oligarchs and below them were the gangsters.

When I was at the club, Shakhtar's president was Akhat Bragin, who was blown up inside his own stadium in a bomb attack in October 1995. He and his entourage had just entered the VIP box to watch a match when eleven pounds of explosives were detonated by remote control. Bragin was identified by his gold Rolex watch found on a dismembered arm.

It was a turf war, a mafia hit. The man who succeeded him was his friend, Rinat Akhmetov, a miner's son made very, very good, who always used to tell Bragin, 'Why do you spend so much money on this football club?'

After Bragin's assassination, Akhmetov felt duty bound to take over Shakhtar. He became Ukraine's richest man and poured in the kind of money that Bragin could only have dreamed about. He built the Donbass Arena, which cost £200m, and a new training ground.

When the stadium was opened in 2009, just after they had beaten Werder Bremen to win the UEFA Cup, Shakhtar invited everyone who had played or worked for the club to its official opening. They served red caviar, black caviar and special Italian wine. It was like being in dreamland; I hadn't tasted wine this good even when I was in Italy, playing for Fiorentina.

The Donbass Arena may be abandoned because of the civil war but it says something about how Shakhtar and maybe Akhmetov are regarded that, although Donetsk airport, which was a beautiful structure, has been completely destroyed, the two sides have tried to avoid hitting the football stadium. It has been struck by some stray shells but is still largely intact.

Most people in Donetsk are trapped between two sides. The Donbass region with its coal and minerals is too valuable for Ukraine to let go. Most of the people who live in Donetsk are ethnically Russian and some things that the Ukrainian government did – like insisting that school lessons be taught only in Ukrainian – simply encouraged the breakaway.

The Donbass might end up as a semi-independent state, connected to Ukraine but governing itself – like the relationship between Monaco and France. But unless there are some serious talks and a desire to stop the shooting, it will all drag on.

I have some friends who are still in Donetsk and they say that you can still hear bombs going off and shooting in the street. The odd shell reaches the city centre. People who once lived alongside each other, trying to kill each other; that is what civil war means.

4
NATIONAL ANTHEMS

I PLAYED FOR THREE NATIONS IN MY INTERNATIONAL career, although my team-mates were usually the same people. I played for the Soviet Union and for Russia. In between, there was something called the Confederation of Independent States, who took part in the 1992 European Championships before the component parts of the Soviet Union all went their own way.

In 1990 the USSR played its last World Cup. It had bid to host the tournament but had lost out to Italy. Having finished second in the European Championships in 1988, Valery Lobanovsky was the manager once more but there was not the same success. By the time Cameroon were defeated 4–0 in the final group game we had been eliminated.

I was not part of Lobanovksy's squad but being part of the Soviet

Union's Under-21 side meant I felt close to them. We were a good team: Dmitri Kharine was in goal, Aleksandar Mostovoi was in midfield with me and we had Igor Kolyranov up front. We would become the last Soviet football team to win a trophy.

If we were good, the team we beat to win the 1990 European Under-21 Championships was a brilliant one. Like the Soviet Union, Yugoslavia was a country that did not have long left. It had an astonishingly good team – Davor Suker, Robert Jarni, Alen Boksic, Zvonimir Boban and Robert Prosinecki.

We beat them 4–2 in the first leg in Sarajevo and won the second leg 3–1 in Simferopol in the Crimea. I scored the third and final goal. Our manager, Vladimir Rodionov, had promised we would be paid our bonuses in dollars, which was a tremendous incentive. It was those games, rather than my performances for Shakhtar Donetsk, that brought me to Manchester United's attention.

By the time we won the trophy in October 1990, I had someone to spend the dollars on. I had met Inna in the summer. I'd come home from Donetsk to visit my mother in Kirovograd. Sergei Palchikov was one of the best swimmers in the Soviet Union and, like me, was a graduate of the Kharkov academy.

He introduced me to Inna. She was seventeen, very beautiful and was an accomplished pianist. She'd just been voted Miss Kirovograd but when they asked Inna if she'd like to take part in the Miss Ukraine beauty pageant, her mother absolutely refused. She went to medical college instead, although our marriage and my move to Manchester United meant she didn't finish the course.

By the time I joined Manchester United, in May 1991, things were changing very fast in the USSR. In August there was a coup. The old Communists who ran the KGB and the Ministry of Defence tried to stop the disintegration of the Soviet Union. They arrested Mikhail Gorbachev and put tanks on the streets of Moscow.

Boris Yeltsin, who was prime minister of Russia, famously stood on a tank and argued with the soldiers, whom he then persuaded not to storm the Russian Parliament, which was called the Bely Dom or the White House. The coup collapsed and with it the Soviet Union.

I wasn't worried about my mother. She was in faraway Kirovograd and there had barely been a shot fired in Moscow. What did I think? By then nobody knew what to think.

In November, the Soviet Union played its final match, a European Championship qualifier in Cyprus. We won 3–0 and I scored its last ever goal, a rebound from the edge of the area.

Gorbachev resigned on Christmas Day and the country just dissolved. I found myself playing for the Confederation of Independent States at the 1992 European Championships. Even though they had qualified, Yugoslavia were not represented in Sweden. The country was being torn apart by civil war.

After Euro 92 I was offered the chance to play for either Russia or Ukraine and I could also have chosen Lithuania, where my father was born. I chose Russia. It felt like the natural successor to the USSR and, if I were to play for Ukraine where I'd grown up, I would have had to wait for Euro 96 qualifiers before I would have been allowed to play competitive internationals (the Football Federation of Ukraine wasn't recognised in time for them to compete in qualifying for the 1994 World Cup). By then, I would have been 27 and there was no telling whether Ukraine would have qualified for them.

They did not actually qualify for a major tournament until the 2006 World Cup when my playing career was coming to an end. I wasn't the only Ukrainian who decided to throw in their lot with Russia and we all did it for the same reason.

I was living in Altrincham, playing for Manchester United, when my decision was announced and soon I was receiving hate mail and death threats, accusing me of being a traitor to my country. They were never signed.

The biggest beneficiary of the break-up of the Soviet Union was Spartak Moscow. If you were from Ukraine or some of the other former Soviet republics and you wanted to continue playing international football, the obvious choice was to say you wanted to play for Russia. Playing in Moscow would help with that and Spartak were very good at offering contracts to the best Ukrainian footballers.

Spartak were Moscow's biggest team. They were popular because, unlike Dynamo, Torpedo or CSKA, they were not connected to a part of the Soviet state. After the collapse, they became hugely successful, winning the Russian Premier League for nine seasons in a row.

In 2000, they signed a huge sponsorship deal with Russia's largest petrochemical company, Lukoil. It should have made them utterly dominant but for sixteen years they failed to win the Russian Premier League. In 2017 the curse was broken.

In Sweden we competed for the first and the last time as the Confederation of Independent States. It was my first major tournament. We were not a nation and we had no national anthem, which was weird when you were standing out in the middle listening to the other team having theirs played.

When we got home, the Russians, Georgians and Ukrainians that made up the squad would go our separate ways. There was plenty of intrigue and stories that if you paid money to certain people you would get selected for the CIS.

Despite all that, we did not play badly. In Norrkoping we would have beaten the Germans but for a last-minute penalty from Thomas Hassler. We drew our second game 0–0, against Holland, a re-run of the 1988 final.

On the final whistle, we knew that if we beat Scotland, who were already eliminated, we would qualify for the semi-finals. Our preparations for the match in Norrkoping were poor and when the game kicked off we were not mentally ready.

Two members of our squad, Alexei Mikhailichenko and Oleg Kuznetsov, played for Glasgow Rangers and our management seemed to think that, because of this, the Scotland players would not try too hard. When we heard the Scottish players had been out all night partying because they knew they had no chance of going through, we were even more confident.

We were deluded. Seeing your opponents going easy on you might have happened in a league game in Russia, if you were coming up against players you knew, but there was no way that footballers like Brian McClair and Ally McCoist were just going to let us win. Scotland beat us 3–0.

I went home to see my mother but my Manchester United team-mate Peter Schmeichel stayed rather longer. Denmark, who had not qualified for Euro 92 but were invited because the civil war meant Yugoslavia could not compete, ended up winning the title.

In 1991 the last ever Soviet League got under way. It would be won by CSKA Moscow. Shakhtar would have a moderate season that would see us finish twelfth out of sixteen. I had two agents, Rune Hauge and Grigori Essaoulenko. Hauge looked after foreign business and Essaoulenko advised me nearer home.

Hauge represented Schmeichel and he told Alex Ferguson that, if he wanted a winger, he could provide him with some videos of me in action. Ferguson was sent a tape of me playing against Italy in a 0–0 draw in Rome. Ferguson was sufficiently intrigued by this to go to Frankfurt in March 1991 to watch the Soviet Union lose narrowly to Germany, who were then world champions.

I only knew about this afterwards. The first inkling I had that I would be leaving Donetsk was when our manager, Valery Yaremchenko, called me and asked if I would be interested in playing abroad.

He said there were English and Greek teams who would like to have a look at me. From the start I knew Yaremchenko and Shakhtar would be well rewarded if they could arrange a transfer with a club in the West. They wanted me to go.

I was told I would be flying to Manchester without being told which club I would be talking to. On the plane I thought it could be City or United or it could even be Liverpool or Everton. It wasn't until I was met at the airport and taken to Old Trafford, where I had my first meeting with Alex Ferguson, that I knew I would be discussing a contract with Manchester United.

The first thing he said to me was: 'Have you brought your boots?' I hadn't. I thought we would just be talking but Ferguson said he wanted us to go to the Cliff, which was Manchester United's training ground at the time, and watch me play.

He told me there was a sports shop down the road and that I should go and get myself a pair. I was really particular about my boots, so much so that I always insisted on cleaning them myself, which came as a surprise to Norman Davies, who was Manchester

United's kit man. I found a pair of boots but the ones I used in Donetsk were moulded. These were just uncomfortable.

With Ferguson watching, I played really badly and, when I took the boots off in the changing rooms, my feet were covered in blisters. Ferguson must have had faith in his judgement because I was offered a contract there and then.

I flew back to Donetsk and had two weeks to sort everything out before going back to Manchester. One of the things I had to arrange was my wedding to Inna. I signed the contract in April and was married on 22 June. I then had to arrange a temporary working visa – a work permit would take much longer to come through.

Inna had to travel to Moscow, 750 miles away, to arrange a visa of her own, which was a really tough process that took a month. The West was more of a shock for Inna than it was for me. I was four years older and football had taken me around Europe so I knew roughly what to expect, but I was still staggered when we walked into a supermarket and saw the abundance of choice on offer. In our shops, there was so little. The other thing I found difficult to get used to was that in England every sink seemed to have a separate hot and cold tap. I was used to mixer taps.

The Russia I was leaving behind was becoming a violent and unpredictable place. The mafia were everywhere, there were regular shootings and score-settlings and by contrast Manchester in 1991 seemed a quiet, almost relaxing environment to find yourself in. You could walk the streets at night without looking over your shoulder.

They gave me an interpreter, George Scanlan, who worked at the John Moores University in Liverpool, and he went with me everywhere. The first English phrase I learned was 'training starts at ten'. Whenever I was asked anything I would reply: 'No problem.'

My Soviet driving licence only allowed me to drive in England for three months so I had to do a British driving test. George sat in the back and relayed the examiner's instructions to me. The examiner kept turning round because he thought George was prompting me.

George was an amazing man. He died during the writing of this book and his friendship is a memory I will always treasure. He had an astonishing gift for languages including Russian, Chinese and Arabic, which are some of the most difficult to learn.

He also spoke French and translated for Eric Cantona and because Eric's English was not very good he travelled a lot with Manchester United, which helped me. I think Ferguson wanted George around because he was a good influence on Eric. Sometimes, if George was translating for both of us, he would turn to Cantona and tell him something in Russian.

George knew his football, too. He had played youth-team football with Ronnie Moran, who became Liverpool's great assistant manager under Bill Shankly and Bob Paisley. He had managed Marine, a non-league club on Merseyside, and interpreted in two World Cups – for the Soviet Union in 1966 and for England in 1990.

He came everywhere with me. He was allowed into the dressing room at Old Trafford and, if I were a substitute, George would sit on the bench to relay any instructions. Once, when Ferguson really screamed at me, George took me into another room and shouted at me in Russian. Other times he would spare my feelings.

Sometimes, Ferguson would say something that I suspected was quite cutting. I would ask George what he'd said and he'd reply: 'The manager thinks you're playing well.'

George wasn't the only one who tried to teach me some English.

Whenever a foreign footballer comes into a dressing room, he will be taught how to swear. I've seen exactly the same thing with Brazilian players when I have been managing in Russia. They also taught me the correct way to address the manager of Manchester United.

Almost the first time I came across Alex Ferguson in the corridors of the Cliff, he said to me, 'All right, Andrei, how's it going?'

I smiled at him and replied, 'Fuck off, Scottish bastard.'

Ferguson stopped dead in his tracks and then began to smile as he heard laughter echoing down the corridor, while I stood there bewildered.

Volkswagen were sponsoring Manchester United at the time so they arranged an Audi for me. The problem was it was an automatic rather than the manual that I was used to and not long after my driving test I crashed it. I was so embarrassed that I didn't want anyone at the club seeing it. I was terrified United would fine me, tell me to pay for the repairs – or worse, take the car away from me.

We had designated parking slots at the Cliff but so that nobody saw the dents, I parked it half a mile away and walked in. I bumped into Jim McGregor, the club physio, who wondered why I appeared to have been walking across Manchester to train. I told him what had happened and he said, 'Don't worry, I'll tell them to take it away and we'll get you a new one.'

Footballers in Manchester, I thought, had an easier life than those in Donetsk.

Every facet of my life was changing. In the West I had to act differently, think differently and dress differently.

One advantage that Manchester had was that there were a lot of people of Ukrainian descent who lived nearby in Oldham and the city also had a Belarussian community. There were some footballers

from what had been the Soviet Union in Britain. Alexei Mikhailichenko, who had been one of Dynamo Kiev's stars when I joined
the club, was with Glasgow Rangers. Another of the Kiev greats,
Sergei Baltacha, was also in Scotland, playing for St Johnstone.
Dmitri Kharine became Chelsea's goalkeeper in 1992 and would
play against me in the FA Cup final two years later. We would
phone each other for advice or for a bit of support or some news
from the old country.

We fared better than one of my team-mates from Shakhtar
Donetsk, who had joined the exodus from the ruins of the Soviet
Union. Sergei Scherbakov had gone not to Britain but to Portugal,
where he had been signed by Bobby Robson at Sporting Lisbon. He
was an attacking midfielder and Robson had persuaded Shakhtar
to allow him to play for Sporting in a pre-season friendly against
Lyons. It took Robson ten minutes to decide to sign him.

When, in December 1993, Sporting Lisbon sacked Robson the
players held a party to say goodbye to their manager, who was leaving them with the club second in the Portuguese Primeira Liga.

Scherbakov drove home without wearing a seatbelt, and was
involved in a collision that propelled him through the roof of his
car and smashed his spine. Sergei has spent the rest of his life in
a wheelchair, although that has not stopped him campaigning
for disabled charities or even working as a youth-team scout. He
should have been one of the great midfielders of his time.

Some of those who came to the Premier League later did not
do themselves justice. Andriy Shevchenko made a great mistake
exchanging AC Milan for Chelsea. In Italy he was number one,
an absolutely outstanding centre-forward who was adored at the
San Siro. He had won the Champions League with Milan in 2003
and Serie A and the Ballon D'Or the following year. There was no

reason for him to move to London.

He agreed the transfer to please his wife, Kristen, who is an American model and would probably have been more comfortable in London than Milan.

Before she met Andriy, Kristen had dated one of Silvio Berlusconi's sons. It was at the time when Berlusconi was mixing football and high politics and it's fair to say he didn't like her much. Berlusconi became godfather to their son, Jordan, but a move to Chelsea would have put some distance between her and the Berlusconis, which could only have pleased Kristen.

Jose Mourinho didn't want Andriy but Berlusconi and Roman Abramovich had decided to do the deal for £30m and when those two decide a deal it gets done. However, it was Mourinho who decided whether or not Shevchenko would play and that's why he kept being sidelined. Mourinho couldn't say it openly but if ever Shevchenko gave him cause for doubt or a reason to drop him, he would be on the bench.

For a footballer, being signed by the chairman and not the manager can leave you in a dead-end street. When I agreed to join Southampton in 2002, it was precisely the same. The man who signed me was the chairman, Rupert Lowe. His manager, Gordon Strachan, didn't want me. I could see that the first time I met him, which is why I didn't play.

Jordi Cruyff's transfer to Manchester United was similar. The club was put under a bit of pressure to take him on the basis he was Johan's son and it would be good to have a Cruyff playing at Old Trafford. Johan was the instigator of the transfer but Alex Ferguson was never entirely convinced by the deal and when Jordi didn't start well at Manchester United he found it hard to win his place back.

Shevchenko was nearly thirty when he came to Stamford Bridge; there were injuries, a new style of play and competition from Didier Drogba. I think the Shevchenkos enjoyed living in London but for the sake of his career he should have stayed in Milan.

There was a lot expected of Andrei Arshavin when he came to Arsenal after helping to take Zenit St Petersburg to the UEFA Cup in 2008 but he wasn't physically ready for the Premier League when he arrived. The deal was done by Alisher Usmanov, who owned 30 per cent of the club, and I think he used his own money to secure the deal because Zenit and Arsenal could not agree a price.

There was a lot of expectation weighing on him and Arshavin found that hard. He was lucky he signed for Arsenal because the kind of football Arsene Wenger played suited him. Had Arshavin gone somewhere else, he would have been in serious trouble early on.

When foreign players arrive in the Premier League, they are asked how they plan to cope with the physicality of English football. It is not a matter of being able to cope with an elbow in the face or a heavy tackle. The question is can you play eighty minutes at a high tempo? The ideal, of course, is ninety, but eighty is fine. Arshavin could play forty.

It is not always a given that players from Russia and Ukraine have had difficulties with the tempo. I enjoyed my first full season at Manchester United because the aggressive, attacking style was just what Valery Lobanovsky had demanded at Dynamo Kiev.

When Oleg Luzhny joined Arsenal from the Kiev side that Lobanovsky had taken to the semi-finals of the Champions League in 1999, his reaction after his first training session was: 'Is that it?' He said that, compared with what he was used to at Dynamo Kiev, Arsene Wenger's training session had been little more than a warm-up.

The problem Roman Pavlyuchenko had at Tottenham was that he was seldom physically fit and had constant problems with his back. He started well enough but the injuries dragged him down and sometimes he played when he should not have done.

The first question Lobanovsky asked of a player was whether he was fit enough. It didn't matter how skilful he was or what impact he might have on the game, Lobanovsky would only select players he thought could complete a football match.

When I met English people they always wanted to know what it was really like in Russia. Half a century of the Cold War had made people very suspicious of the Soviet Union but at the same time they were fascinated by the country.

The only knowledge some English people seemed to have of Russia came from James Bond movies. After the Soviet Union collapsed, that changed. Where once every Russian was a spy, now he was a member of the Russian mafia.

I arrived at Manchester United at roughly the same time that Peter Schmeichel did and the club put us up at a small but very nice family-run hotel in Sale called the Amblehurst, whose owner was good friends with Bryan Robson. He and Steve Bruce used to go there for a drink and there was a bar nearby called the Little B that they used to use. So I had three team-mates who I knew outside the Cliff and Old Trafford and when Peter Schmeichel found his own place he invited us over.

I made my debut for Manchester United on 11 May 1991, the day after the club was given clearance to play me. It was at Crystal Palace and it was not a game to remember. We lost 3–0 and, because Manchester United were due to play Barcelona in the Cup Winners'

Cup final on the Wednesday, Ferguson fielded a weakened team.

Most of those who played at Selhurst Park would not be playing against Barcelona in Rotterdam and those that were had their minds on bigger things. I played in midfield alongside Darren Ferguson, the manager's son. Like me, Darren was not picked to play in the final at the De Kuip. Ferguson was not the kind of person to show favouritism.

I had not been signed in time to play against Barcelona but I was invited to travel with the squad to Rotterdam. I was told that it was the first European final Manchester United had played since they won the European Cup at Wembley in 1968. I thought that strange. I thought a club like Manchester United would have had more finals.

Barcelona had a fantastic team, managed by Johan Cruyff, with players like Ronald Koeman and Michael Laudrup, but Mark Hughes scored twice in the rain and although Koeman got a goal back it was not enough. I had been a Manchester United player for a week and I had seen them win a European trophy.

When we got back to our hotel on the outskirts of Rotterdam, they had laid on an enormous buffet and what seemed to me to be a lot of alcohol. We had a long, long party. I wasn't used to so much drink and when I woke up it was with a tremendous hangover.

Then, when we returned to Manchester, we were paraded in an open-topped bus around the city. It was the first time I had come across this. If you won a trophy or a cup in the Soviet Union, you would be presented with a medal at your own stadium and perhaps there would be a little tour of the ground to greet the fans. There was no question of touring the streets of the city.

The day made a huge impression on me. The fans lined the

sides of the roads with flags and banners. There were huge crowds around Old Trafford. It was that day, more than anything I had read or been told about Manchester United, that made me realise the size of the club I had joined.

5
BITTERSWEET CHAMPION

MANCHESTER UNITED MAY HAVE BEEN A MUCH bigger club than either Dynamo Kiev or Shakhtar Donetsk but there were some things about it that struck me as a little bit amateurish.

Before every home game in the Soviet Union, we would stay the night at the training ground, which had accommodation for the players, study videos of our opponents and have a meal and a team-talk. For away fixtures we would use a hotel. It was the kind of approach that so fascinated men like Marcello Lippi and Fabio Capello about Soviet football.

But at Old Trafford the pre-match instructions were: 'Drive yourself to the ground at 11.45 for tea, coffee and toast and then 3pm kick-off.' We would be served a meal, usually of chicken and beans, whereas in the Soviet Union the rule was that you wouldn't eat anything for five hours before kick-off. There was so much food I wondered how anyone was going to run.

My first taste of Old Trafford as a player came in August 1991 – just as the tanks were rolling through the streets of Moscow in a last attempt to keep the old Communist system alive. Manchester United were playing Notts County. We won 2–0 and it was my cross that provided one of the goals.

I enjoyed my first season at Manchester United. I adapted quickly because Alex Ferguson's way of playing, with two wingers, was not so very different from Valery Lobanovsky's.

The stadium was fast becoming a building site. The Stretford End was being rebuilt and for a time Old Trafford looked like a smile missing a tooth. The team, too, was being reconstructed.

After we had beaten Barcelona to win the Cup Winners' Cup, Ferguson predicted that Manchester United would finish the season with the league title and we very nearly did. In 1991/92 we won the League Cup and the Super Cup, beating Red Star Belgrade, the European champions, and we should have won the league.

The championship became a straight fight between Manchester United and Leeds. On the way we won the League Cup, beating Nottingham Forest.

The final was not my first time at Wembley. Three years before, in 1989, I had played for Dynamo Kiev in a pre-season tournament that also featured Liverpool, Arsenal and Porto. It made a huge impression on me then and the sense of wonder was even greater when we played Nottingham Forest there.

We won 1-0 with Ryan Giggs slipping the ball through for Brian McClair to score. In November, McClair had also scored the only goal in the Super Cup final, which was supposed to have been

played over two legs but was staged as a single fixture at Old Trafford because the civil war in Yugoslavia made it too dangerous for
Manchester United to travel to Belgrade. Red Star played astonishingly well and yet somehow managed to lose.

Like the night in Rotterdam when we won the Cup Winners'
Cup, the scale of the celebrations after our victory over Nottingham Forest astonished me. This was a team that knew how to party.

Manchester United were leading the table for much of the season
and it made our failure to win the title that much more painful. We
played Leeds three times in eighteen days; once in each of the cup
competitions and once in the league.

We won the cup games but when we beat Leeds 1–0 in the FA
Cup in January, they lost their striker, Lee Chapman, to injury. In
February 1992 they bought Eric Cantona. Leeds lost the first game
he played for them, at Oldham, but they won the title.

In his five years in English football, Cantona won the league five
times. Had he not got himself banned for leaping into the crowd
at Crystal Palace, it would have been six. That is the measure of the
man.

Leeds may have won the title but Manchester United also lost
it. Cantona did not propel them to the title as he propelled United
in 1996 – they picked up fewer points per game in the matches he
played than they did before he arrived. But if Leeds stumbled, we
collapsed. The enemy was exhaustion and what I thought was poor
judgement from Alex Ferguson.

There seemed to be so many games at the end of that season. On
a Thursday, 16 April, we beat Southampton 1–0 at Old Trafford to
go two points clear of Leeds with a game in hand. I scored the goal
but was left out for the fixture at Luton two days later. I could not

understand Ferguson's reasoning because I felt in great form. We could only draw 1–1 at Luton and dropping those two points was critical because it upset our momentum.

Manchester United had a game on Monday, at home to Nottingham Forest; and another on Wednesday at West Ham. We lost them both but, had we beaten Luton, I am still convinced we would have won those two matches.

I played in the defeat at West Ham. They were already relegated but the atmosphere at Upton Park was incredibly intimidating, especially towards Paul Ince because he had left them for Manchester United. They are strange fans at West Ham, very, very aggressive.

By the final whistle we were second, a point behind Leeds with two matches to play. We lost at Liverpool on the Sunday and that was that. It was over.

Ferguson said he was furious at the way West Ham had raised their game to play Manchester United when they had been so bad for so long. 'Obscene', he called it in the press conference, although in the dressing room, where we knew we had lost the title, he was much calmer and more reasoned.

Ferguson must have known that in a one-off football match any team can raise its game, particularly if they are playing Manchester United. And Manchester United are a big, big club; they should be able to cope.

Everyone always wants to beat Manchester United just as in rugby everyone wants to beat the All Blacks. When you put on a Manchester United shirt you have to know the sense of expectation you are pulling on with it.

After the defeat at Anfield, I met their manager, Graeme Souness, who told my interpreter, George Scanlan, to ask me why I had not joined Liverpool. 'Manchester United play too many long balls,' Souness said. 'Here at Liverpool, we play everything along the ground and that would suit you.'

If I adapted well to Ferguson's tactics, adapting to the man himself was more difficult. We were never prepared for his explosions of temper. He would come right up to you, screaming in your face. The players called it 'The Hairdryer' but I always referred to it as 'The Hoover'. The three he tended to pick out were Peter Schmeichel, Steve Bruce and Gary Pallister. Looking back, he singled them out because they could take it.

Because my English was so poor, it didn't really affect me as much as it should have done. Ferguson must have thought I wouldn't understand if he yelled at me. When he did, I often had no idea what he was trying to say. Sometimes, in the dressing room at Old Trafford I would turn to an English player and ask what the manager had said and often the reply would come, out of the corner of his mouth: 'No idea.'

On other occasions you would look up and the teacups would be on the dressing-room floor. Other times, when you did not expect it, he could be lovely to you.

There was one confrontation I will always remember. Ferguson tried to take on Mark Hughes and Hughes would not have it. They were squaring up to each other and Brian Kidd, the assistant manager, was trying to get between them, pleading with them to calm down.

Hughes kept telling Ferguson to fuck off.

Ferguson replied, 'One week's wages.'

'Fuck off.'

'Two weeks' wages.'

'Fuck right off.'

'Three weeks' wages.'

And Kiddo was trying to push them apart, saying, 'Stop, stop. For God's sake; both of you just stop.'

What was so extraordinary about Ferguson's loss of temper was how quickly he calmed down. If we lost, he could be very aggressive. For ten minutes in the dressing room after a defeat all you would hear would be his voice, loudly going back and forth across the room. It was intimidating. It was meant to be.

Once he had said what he wanted to say, his voice would go back to normal and he would treat you as if nothing had happened. If the time was right, he might pour himself a glass of wine and give you one of his smiles. Or, if it were an away game, he might come down to the back of the bus and ask if he could join in the card school.

I preferred it that way. I thought it was good that your manager could tell you exactly what he thought of you rather than bottle it all up. The other thing we appreciated was that Ferguson never, ever went to the press with stories about us. There were some managers that did and they very quickly lost the respect of their players. Being in a team is the same thing as being in a family. You would say things to your team-mates, confide in them, tell them your secret thoughts, in a way you never would to an outsider.

You would also criticise them in language you would never use to an outsider. But, if someone outside the team, outside the family, used the same words, you wouldn't take it. They weren't part of the team, so they weren't allowed to criticise it. That, to me, is how a dressing room works.

When I first went to Manchester United there was quite a bit of interest in me from the press and television in the Soviet Union but after the break-up the interviews and articles began to dry up. Russia was so beset by financial problems, by the mafia and the murders and the settling of scores that accompanied the end of the Soviet Union, that it became very difficult to justify sending out a television crew just to interview someone who played football for Manchester United.

I would send money home to my mother in Kirovograd and when Yevgenia came over to Manchester for a visit she was amazed by the place. Having had to queue all her adult life, she was astonished by the sheer quantity of produce in the supermarkets. 'But the shops are full of food and clothes and everything,' Mum would say to me. 'And the people are so nice. The staff in the shops actually smile at you.' I told her that you got used to these things very quickly.

Compared to what I was used to in the Soviet Union or what I became used to in Italy, there was not a great deal of time spent discussing tactics in England. Ferguson had his set way of playing that in my four years at Old Trafford did not change that much. If he wanted you to do something different, he would call you into his office at the Cliff or take you to one side after a training session.

Ferguson would have thought that by the time you started playing for Manchester United you should know your game tactically. He was probably right. Talking to players about tactics tends to be more successful lower down the divisions where footballers are less sure of their jobs and their abilities.

When you came to Manchester United, you would be given an induction. They would take you to the museum, walk you round Old Trafford and tell you stories about George Best, Denis Law and Sir Matt Busby. They were really aware of their own history. We all knew about the 1968 European Cup and we knew from the very start that the one thing that had been missing from Manchester United's history for so long was the league title.

The second full season in England should have been easy. I felt I had established myself in Alex Ferguson's teams.

The partnership with Ryan Giggs had been one of the highlights of the season and I loved playing with Giggsy. In my first season we had a bet as to who would score first. He won by over three months.

He was eighteen when the 1992/93 season began but he was a star on the pitch and off it, the most glamorous man at Old Trafford. This was before David Beckham.

I had made friends, particularly with Bryan Robson. I didn't know his dad was a lorry driver as mine had been. He had taken me to his house and to Chester races and to a Paul Simon concert. I wouldn't say I had close friends at Manchester United but I used to hang out with Lee Sharpe and Inna was with me in Altrincham.

I thought, wrongly as it turned out, that my second full season at Old Trafford would be the one that made my reputation. I had come back from the European Championship and felt I had played well against Germany and Holland, two very difficult opponents. Against Holland in Gothenburg, I had been used in a much more defensive role and done well against Bryan Roy. I was ready for the new season.

After three games all my confidence seemed completely misplaced. Manchester United had taken one point from their first three games, were twentieth in the new Premier League table and I was out of the team.

We had lost to Sheffield United and Everton and managed a 1–1 draw with Ipswich. If you added the results at the end of the

1991/92 season, it meant Manchester United had lost five and drawn two of their last eight games. Ferguson had to act.

At the time, I was furious to be dropped, especially since Ferguson now seemed to be favouring Lee Sharpe. But I think he wanted Manchester United to tighten up, to be more defensive, and I was one of those who had to go.

I have been a manager and when it comes to team selection the manager, the trainer, the coach, call him what you will, has to be backed. It is his job on the line, his neck on the block. If I had been manager of Manchester United then, I would have dropped myself.

I would, however, have picked myself for the UEFA Cup tie against Torpedo Moscow. It was a game I was desperate to play in.

I was at least part of the squad that flew to Russia in September 1992. Funnily enough, I was the only player who had a problem with his visa. Ken Merrett, who was then the club secretary, had been given the task of organising the visas but while I had an entry visa, I didn't have one that allowed me to leave.

It was sorted out and the hotel we stayed in, not far from the Olympic Stadium, which is now called the Luzhniki, was a symbol of the new Russia emerging under Boris Yeltsin. It was new, it was sleek and it was European-owned.

We were all given a tour of the Kremlin and Red Square. We all posed for photographs with old Soviet memorabilia. Giggsy bought a fur hat and even Alex Ferguson had his photo taken wearing a general's cap.

It was astonishing to think that sixteen years later he would win the European Cup in this same city managing the same team – a team in which Ryan Giggs would be playing. He didn't take the opportunity to buy the full general's uniform which was on sale in

Red Square.

I was disappointed with his tactics in Moscow. The Russian national manager, Anatoly Bishovets, and my old manager at Shakhtar Donetsk, Valery Yaremchenko, had come to the small, open Torpedo Stadium to watch me play.

In wet, freezing conditions, they watched me sit on the bench while Manchester United lost the tie on penalties. Ferguson played Danny Wallace in my position on the right wing and then substituted him before half-time. Mark Hughes was sent off and Torpedo Moscow, who had held United 0–0 at Old Trafford, held out for another goalless draw and then won the penalty shoot-out.

The problems continued when we tried to make our way back to Manchester. Ken Merrett, who had organised the visas for everybody else, forgot his own when we tried to fly back and was detained for several days.

I thought this was really serious but when we got on the plane and drinks were handed round, the chairman, Martin Edwards, stood up and asked the passengers to raise a glass 'to absent friends'. It took several days for Ken to make his way back to Manchester and in the meantime the staff had jokily tied ribbons round his office door and lit candles to 'remember him by'.

Until that autumn of 1992 everything in my game had come quickly and easily. I didn't get my place back until the end of October when we played Wimbledon at Old Trafford. I knew I wasn't ready for it. It was a terrible game, I played terribly and we lost again, 1–0. 'What the hell was that?' Ferguson said to me after the match. 'You didn't play at all.'

Manchester United had by then climbed to seventh, six points behind Norwich and Blackburn. With me in the team they had taken one point from four games. I had to change my attitude and my performance if I was to have a future at Manchester United.

Second seasons are always dangerous. Perhaps I had relaxed too much. I had shown Manchester United what I was capable of in 1991/92 and I may have felt I had proved my ability. I was also no longer an unknown quantity. Defenders were becoming used to me and my moves. Some people react well to being dropped and some don't. I was bringing less of myself into training.

I was also lonely. I was a foreigner, one of the few in the Premier League, and I spoke little English. Being part of the team, the chatter in the dressing room, the build-up to the match, all made feel at the centre of things. I was lost without it.

In my six weeks out of the side I had thought that Ferguson had made up his mind about me and there was no point trying to change his opinion in training. I would turn up, do what was asked of me and go home.

When the days out of the side turned into weeks, I realised I would have to force him to pick me. I would train so hard and so well, Ferguson would have no choice but to change his mind.

It didn't go quite according to plan. We had just finished a training session when the manager took me to one side and said I would be playing in the reserves.

'No, I am not going to do it,' I said. 'I have not come from Donetsk to play for Manchester United reserves.' Steve Bruce shot me one of his looks. He didn't say anything but the meaning was clear: I should be very careful what I said next.

When Ferguson told me he wanted to carry on the conversation in his office, I wasn't careful what I said. His office was nothing flash but it had a big window that overlooked the training pitches.

He was always watching us.

'Are you joking about not playing for the reserves?' he said.

'No, I am not joking. You can fine me or you can transfer me. You can send me to Siberia but I am never going to play for Manchester United reserves.'

He lost his temper. Completely. 'You can rot on the bench then.'

The next day I trained with the youth team and then I trained with the reserves. Meanwhile Ferguson got on with turning Manchester United into champions. He did this by signing Eric Cantona.

I liked to compare Cantona to David Ginola, who would join Newcastle a couple of years later. They were both amazing individual talents but Cantona was more of a team player while Ginola often played for himself. Ginola was a good footballer but Cantona was a great one.

In the dressing room he was very quiet, very reserved. When he first moved to Manchester United, Cantona still lived in Yorkshire and then he moved into a hotel by the motorway that links Manchester and Leeds. It was a small hotel. It wasn't luxurious but he chose it because it was convenient.

Eric wasn't much interested in luxury. He was also a man who was happy in his own company. Peter Schmeichel, who would room with him on away trips, was probably closer to him than any of us.

It was Boxing Day before I had a chance to play alongside Cantona. We were playing Sheffield Wednesday at Hillsborough and were three down with 28 minutes left. We fought back to draw 3–3. Cantona scored the equaliser and I was brought on as a substitute.

I felt I had played quite well but I didn't start a game until January when we won 3–1 at Queens Park Rangers. I was being considered for the away matches but not the games at Old Trafford.

I didn't even make the bench for the game everyone remembers, the return match against Sheffield Wednesday when Steve Bruce scored the winner in the sixth minute of stoppage time and Ferguson and Brian Kidd ran on to the pitch and leapt into each other's arms.

I made the party at Bruce's house when Aston Villa lost to Oldham and Manchester United knew they would be champions for the first time since 1967. We were four points ahead of Aston Villa who were at Oldham on the Sunday. We played Blackburn the following day.

We were brought in for some light training on the Sunday morning but Ferguson announced he would not be watching the game. He would be playing golf and he advised none of us to watch the match either.

Obviously we did and we began gravitating towards Steve's house as it became clear Oldham were going to win.

Nobody seemed to care we would be playing Blackburn the following evening. I was one of the earlier ones to leave but some were still going just before dawn broke over Manchester.

Incredibly, we won that game, but what was almost as strange was that Ferguson's team talk was the same as he always gave before a match. There was hardly a mention of the fact we had just become champions. Since we all knew that this was his burning ambition, his control was amazing. He was just focused on beating Blackburn.

He took me aside and told me that he knew I had not had a good season but that he would bring me on as a substitute so I could enjoy the sound of Old Trafford celebrating the league title at last.

After the game, we were introduced to Sir Matt Busby, George

Best, Denis Law and Bobby Charlton, the men who had won Manchester United their last title, two years before I was born.

Of course I was happy that Manchester United were champions but I was disappointed I had not contributed more. For the first time since I was starting out as a young footballer in Kirovograd, I had doubted myself.

I went to see Ferguson in his office and I asked to leave Manchester United. In December, not long after Cantona had made his full debut in a 1–0 win over Norwich, Yaremchenko had come to Altrincham to see me. He had talked with Ferguson about my future and told me my manager had been pretty negative about me. Ferguson had complained about my habit of not lifting my head as I ran, my poor crossing and my lack of understanding of the English game.

I had come on as a substitute at Chelsea on the day Cantona scored his first goal for Manchester United and felt I'd played quite well; I pointed out that the same criticisms about not understanding the English game had been levelled against Cantona when he first joined Leeds. As a winger, I thought the flat back four, which was a trademark of the English game, should suit me.

However, Yaremchenko pointed out that the 1994 World Cup was on the horizon and, if I wanted to be part of the Russian squad, I had to play more. The only realistic way of doing that was to leave.

Looking back, it would have been in Yaremchenko's interests for me to leave because Shakhtar were entitled to a big percentage of my transfer fee if I were sold on. At the time, I agreed with him, I had to get out of Manchester.

I had expected another confrontation with Ferguson but I thought that at the end of it he would relent and allow me to leave.

Manchester United had qualified for the European Cup and at that time UEFA only allowed a team to play three foreigners. As a Russian who did not have the manager's confidence, I thought he would consider me surplus to requirements.

However, when I went to see him, he was relaxed and friendly. He told me I should stay at Manchester United, that I would have more opportunities next season, especially since the club was now competing for the European Cup. He told me to go on holiday and bring him a tin of caviar when I came back. I decided to stay.

6
MY BOYS

THERE WAS ANOTHER REASON WHY I FELT SO ANGRY and out of sorts during my second season at Manchester United. Inna and I had lost our baby.

Inna had become pregnant and by Christmas 1992 we knew she was carrying a baby boy. It put being out of the team into perspective. We were spending a better Christmas in Altrincham than the rest of my family were in what was now the independent state of Ukraine.

It was when I arrived home from London after we had played Queens Park Rangers in mid-January that things began to go wrong. I had called her from the team hotel before the game and everything was fine but by the time I got back Inna knew something wasn't right.

She could not feel the baby in her womb. There was no movement, no kicking, nothing. The next day we went to the hospital for a scan and they told us the baby had died in the womb and she would have to have an operation to remove the foetus. I was allowed to sleep in the same room as Inna. She was traumatised. They gave us the baby to hold and all we could do was cry.

Alex Ferguson called straight away to see if there was anything he could do. I was due to play on the Saturday, at home to Brighton in the FA Cup, but he told me not to concern myself with football. My place was at home with Inna.

Manchester United's chaplain, John Boyers, came to our home to offer counselling and practical help, like arranging the funeral. Bryan Robson and Steve Bruce called round and said the whole squad wanted to attend the service. In the end we thought it best if just Brian McClair, who was my room-mate on away trips, came to the funeral along with Alex Ferguson and Brian Kidd. We had not chosen a Christian name for our boy. The gravestone said simply: 'Baby Boy'.

I had to force myself back into football. I had lost all desire for the game. Flowers kept arriving at our house along with letters from other couples who had suffered a similar tragedy. Eventually, I went back to the Cliff and decided to throw myself into my work. It was the only way. Inna became pregnant again and in December 1993 she gave birth to a boy. We called him Andrei.

Later, when I was living in Scotland, we had a daughter, Eva. She supports Manchester United but Andrei became an Everton fan.

I thought he might make it as a footballer but it requires a lot of dedication, work and commitment and sometimes teenagers find that difficult. It was hard for him because the football school was the other side of the city and by then Inna and I had separated. The sport he really enjoys is rugby.

The Manchester United side that began the new season as champions was an immensely powerful unit. Alex Ferguson had strengthened the side by buying Roy Keane from Nottingham Forest and we were becoming an aggressive, confident team that was as comfortable away from home as we were at Old Trafford. It was such a good side – Schmeichel, Bruce, Pallister, Parker, Keane, Ince, Cantona, Robson, Giggs, Hughes – that if you fast-forwarded that team twenty years it would still win the Premier League.

It was full of incredibly strong personalities; men who said exactly what they thought and were not afraid of an argument. In some circumstances this would be a recipe for disaster but because they were all united by respect for Ferguson it worked. He was the man who knitted what could be a fearsome dressing room together.

If I had to pick a fantasy team of the best footballers I played with in my career, the vast majority of that side would be the one that won the Double for Manchester United in 1994. There might be one or two exceptions. I would have Gabriel Batistuta as my centre-forward. Oleg Luzhny would be right-back and Vladimir Bessonov, who anchored the defence for both Dynamo Kiev and the Soviet Union, would partner Steve Bruce at centre-half but the rest would be the boys of 1993/94.

I played in the first game, a 2–0 win at Norwich, which did not surprise me because the previous season I had played most of my games away from home, but I kept my place for the second at Old Trafford. We beat Sheffield United 3–0. We won five of our first six games and, after that, we hardly faltered.

It was the best team I ever played in and what I remember about it was how much enjoyment we got out of the game. If you enjoy football, you tend not to get bogged down by weaker teams, you always trust yourself to win. You could see that quality in the great Barcelona teams and there was something of that in that Manchester United side. If we met a team that scored first against us, we didn't panic. We knew we had enough resources to come back.

The Manchester derby in November was proof of that. The team had just returned from Istanbul, where we had been knocked out of the Champions League by Galatasaray. Because of the UEFA rule that said teams could only field three foreigners, I hadn't travelled to Turkey. Eric Cantona, Keane and Peter Schmeichel were ahead of me. I only heard about the violence that had been inflicted on our fans, the 'Welcome to Hell' banners and the scenes of Cantona fighting with the police.

A year later, I would face Galatasaray at the Ali Sami Yen. We played out a goalless draw in the single most intimidating atmosphere in which I have played – and I include Celtic Park in that.

On the wing close to the stands at the Ali Sami Yen, you were a target for all sorts of missiles, you could hear every word they screamed; you could almost smell them. The stands were packed and the chanting began an hour before kick-off.

In 1993 the Manchester United squad had been shocked, unnerved by what confronted them in Istanbul, but I had an inkling of what to expect. When I first went to Turkey with the Soviet Union's Under-21 side, it was rough. When we went out of the hotel, we were given a bodyguard.

The Manchester derby would almost have come as a relief after that and perhaps it was not a surprise that we went two goals down at Maine Road. Ferguson did not panic and neither did his players. Cantona scored twice to equalise but we were not the kind of team that would have been happy with a draw. Keane scored the winner.

Peter Schmeichel was the best keeper I played with in my career. Playing with a great goalkeeper makes such a difference to a team. You concentrate on your own play because you know the opposition will have to do extremely well to score. You don't panic whenever they cross the halfway line, you don't keep glancing over your shoulder. He gave the impression that he had everything under control.

Schmeichel remains the best goalkeeper in the history of Manchester United. David de Gea follows closely behind him. The great Manchester United sides that Ferguson created had, at their core, a great keeper; first Schmeichel and then Edwin van der Sar. De Gea is in that mould. It was not a surprise that Real Madrid should have made such a concerted attempt to take De Gea, but if Jose Mourinho was serious about taking United back to where they were under Ferguson, they had to do everything they could to stop the transfer.

Manchester made Peter Schmeichel. He arrived at the same time as Paul Parker and I did, in 1991. At the time most Manchester United players had little real idea of who he was or what he was like as a person.

One of Manchester United's tactics was to get the ball back into play as quickly as possible and Schmeichel did this by being able to throw the ball sixty or seventy yards. It was far more accurate than just kicking the ball and Peter's strength meant it went nearly as far.

Schmeichel ran his defence with an iron fist and he would scream abuse at Steve Bruce and Gary Pallister. Mostly, they would work really well as a unit but sometimes you would glance around and they would almost be coming to blows with each other.

You would walk into the dressing room after the game and expect Schmeichel and his defenders to have the most astonishing arguments but it was nearly always fine and then they would have a pint together in the players' lounge.

Off the pitch, Schmeichel was much quieter and, if he did try to impose himself in the dressing room, he found there was only one person who mattered there and that was Alex Ferguson.

When you meet Steve Bruce, you think he must be a very nice guy. But he was different on the pitch, where he gave his all, which may be why he got into so many rows with Schmeichel.

In my years playing at Old Trafford I never once saw him turn away from the ball. When I became a manager, I would fine players if they turned their backs on the ball. 'Nobody on the planet has ever been killed by a football, so don't turn your back on it,' I used to shout.

Bruce's eyes were always on the ball and, if he had a lapse of concentration, I cannot remember it. That Steve Bruce never played for England was one of the more surprising things that happened in my time at Manchester United.

Roy Keane was to become one of the great captains of Manchester United once Bryan Robson and Cantona left the club but that season he had just come to Old Trafford. Right from the start you knew how good he was and how high his standards were. He wouldn't make any excuses for himself and he wouldn't accept any from anyone else.

It didn't matter who you were, Keane thought the only reason you should be in the dressing room with him was if you wanted to win. He would even turn on Ryan Giggs if he thought he wasn't playing well. I think he may have been a bit in awe of Cantona but then we all were. If he detected any lack of commitment, he would be on your case. When you played alongside Roy Keane, you needed to be fit and on your toes.

I had left Manchester United by the time Keane became captain but he drove them on. When he was in the dressing room at half-time he would turn on some players if they were not performing but he would also encourage others and pat them on the back. And that meant more because it was from Keane.

To me, he is one of the most important players in the history of Manchester United. The club owes him a lot. It was that unwillingness to lose that took them to so many places.

Perhaps it was coincidence, but my form began to improve in December just after Andrei was born. By the start of 1994 Manchester United were on course for three trophies – the championship, the League Cup and the FA Cup. We won two and lost the League Cup final to Aston Villa.

Schmeichel was suspended against Villa and I was sent off for handling Dalian Atkinson's shot on the line. Had I not done it, they would have scored a third. I watched from the touchline as Dean Saunders scored the penalty that made it 3–1. I would have done it again. Aston Villa might have missed the penalty; we might have scored a late equaliser. We were the sort of side that did score late.

We won the championship easily with 92 points, the highest total by any Manchester United side. There were one or two moments of tension. In January we drew 3–3 with Liverpool at Anfield and Ferguson completely lost his temper with us. He went so over the top that he apologised to us the next day.

He had singled out Peter Schmeichel. He said his kicking had not been good enough and that every time he made a clearance Liverpool had won possession. Schmeichel answered him back and the argument got so out of hand that Schmeichel threatened to quit the club.

The following day, Ferguson gathered us together and told us that the row in the dressing room at Anfield should not have happened. Then he left the room and Schmeichel apologised for his behaviour. What we didn't know was that beforehand Ferguson had called Schmeichel into his office and sacked him. Fortunately for Manchester United, he had then changed his mind.

It was an astonishing match. Liverpool were eighth when we played them and had no hope of winning the championship but even when they were three goals down they were still determined to fight. Ryan Giggs scored a beautiful goal, chipping Bruce Grobbelaar on the run, and when Denis Irwin scored with a free kick we all thought the game was over. By half-time, it was 3–2 and at the finish 3–3. They would not give in.

It was an isolated incident because we seemed predestined to win the championship. Our best performance was a 5–0 win over Sheffield Wednesday. The one concern I had was that the time on the three-year contract I had signed in 1991 was quickly running out.

My sending-off against Aston Villa meant I missed the FA Cup semi-final against Oldham. That was also staged at Wembley and but for a fabulous volley from Mark Hughes in the last minute of extra time Oldham would have won it. The replay was at Maine Road where I scored one of the goals I shall always remember. We were leading 1–0 when I got the ball and cut inside and kept going the length of the 18-yard line without quite knowing what to do next. I saw an opening and shot with my left foot. We ended up winning 4–1.

As the match finished, the Manchester United fans began chanting that I must stay. There had been no public offer of a new contract and some fans started a petition urging the board to give me a new one. There were hundreds of signatures and there was a lovely comment from a 72-year-old pensioner called Mary Wood. She wrote: 'I am an old-age pensioner and I know a good footballer when I see one. Please stay.' The week before the FA Cup final I signed a five-year contract that would see me among the best-paid players at Old Trafford. I was photographed shaking hands with Martin Edwards in the Manchester United chairman's office. It would be in that same office a year later where we would have the row that finished with me leaving the club.

It was a time when salaries were exploding in the Premier League, when the distance between footballers and those who came to watch them suddenly became very wide, at least financially.

The contract I signed with Manchester United in 1991 paid me £120,000 a year. At Old Trafford now most of the first team would reckon to earn that in a week. I was always taught that money was a secondary factor in sport.

When I was at Dynamo Kiev, Valery Lobanovsky told me, 'You concentrate on your football and everything else will come. If you play well and keep playing well, you will get a flat and, after that, you will get a car.'

These days, both in England and in Russia, money seems to be the main motivation for young footballers. They are paid too much, too soon, and then their clubs wonder why they suddenly seem to lack motivation. Both Russia and England have very well-paid young players and an underperforming national team. That cannot be a coincidence. If football is not your first and overwhelming priority, you cannot call yourself a footballer.

Chelsea, who were then managed by Glenn Hoddle and had Dmitri Kharine in goal, had beaten us home and away in the Premier League and we would play them at Wembley for the FA Cup. Before the game, Dmitri and I had discussed the final and we were both thrilled at the thought of it.

Dmitri was one of those goalkeepers who emerged very young. He was 24 when he signed for Chelsea but by then he had already played for three of Moscow's big four clubs – Torpedo, Dynamo and CSKA – and had been part of the Soviet Union side that won the gold medal in the football tournament at the Seoul Olympics. He was our goalkeeper when the Soviet Union won the European Under-21 tournament in 1990.

His career turned on a tragic accident. In June 1991, CSKA Moscow won the Soviet Cup final, beating Torpedo 1–0. The next day, their goalkeeper, Mikhail Yeremin, was killed in a car crash when his tyre exploded and caused him to crash into a bus. Dmitri was a good friend of Mikhail and offered his services to CSKA after talking to Yeremin's parents.

CSKA became the first side to win the Russian Premier League after the break-up of the Soviet Union and they played Johan Cruyff's Barcelona, who were the European champions, in the second round of the Champions League. CSKA drew 1–1 in the Luzhniki and then won 3–2 in the Nou Camp. Barcelona were 2–0 up before CSKA scored three times in the second half to create one of the few great nights in post-Soviet football. The pity was that because of the economic collapse in Russia no television station back home had been able to afford the rights to screen the game.

One influential person did, however, watch it. Chelsea had sent a scout to that game and he recommended Kharine's signing not just on the basis of his performance in Barcelona but from how he approached the warm-up.

A month later, in December 1992, Kharine, his wife Lila and his son Igor exchanged Moscow for London just in time for Christmas. Chelsea had arranged a house for the Kharine family and on his first day of training, while Lila was out shopping, it was broken into. The door was smashed down and £25,000 in cash and jewellery was stolen.

You can't be blasé about Wembley, a place where history and tradition are everywhere. The FA Cup final is an occasion where everything is done beautifully, from the build-up with the military bands to the atmosphere of the game itself and the presentation. Funnily enough, we weren't allowed to talk to the press about how we felt about the occasion because Ferguson had forbidden us to give interviews.

It looked like it might be a close game but we knew we were going to win. There was never any doubt in our minds. This was a Manchester United side at the very top of its game and we fancied ourselves against any team in England. We won 4–0.

The only regret was that Bryan Robson, the man who had really looked after me at Old Trafford and who was leaving at the end of the season to manage Middlesbrough, was not picked for the game. If it had been up to the players, he would have been part of the FA Cup final.

When I came to Manchester, I had little knowledge of our opponents and Bryan would always seek me out and give me little tips about who I would be up against. Inside Old Trafford he had been my greatest supporter.

There was one of the huge parties Manchester United specialised in but I made sure I left early. The next day we would fly back for the parade through the city in front of hundreds of thousands when we would show off the first Double in Manchester United's history. But there was another event on that day, the baptism of our son.

Strangely, most of the members of that great Manchester United side did not go to the United States that summer for the World Cup. England, Wales, France and Denmark had not qualified, which meant no Paul Ince, Mark Hughes, Ryan Giggs, Eric Cantona or Peter Schmeichel.

Roy Keane and Denis Irwin went with the Republic of Ireland and Russia had also qualified, but I did not go. I refused to go.

Although we had lost only one qualifier against Greece, there was a lot of dissatisfaction with the Russian Football Union. Fourteen of our players signed a letter protesting about what we thought were sloppy and unprofessional preparations for the biggest tournament in world football. The hotel for the final qualifying match in Athens was dreadful.

We did not think that the national manager, Pavel Sadyrin, who had been in charge of CSKA Moscow and who had won the last ever Soviet championship, was up to the job and we thought some of the preparations were slapdash. Some of us wanted Anatoly Bishovets, who had managed the Confederation of Independent States in the European Championship, to take Russia to the tournament.

Bishovets was born in Kiev and had played for Dynamo so maybe he was not now thought of as Russian, but we thought him a better manager than Sadyrin. There were some members of the Russian government who shared our opinion. But Sadyrin had a lot of support as well and he was a real intriguer – there were plenty of stories of under-the-table deals surrounding him.

In October 1993, in an attempt to persuade me to play, Sadyrin came to Manchester to see me. There was a lot of pressure on me to change my mind but I had signed the letter and I thought it was the right thing to do to stick by my beliefs. Six of my team-mates stuck with me.

Had the Russian FA appointed Oleg Romantsev, who was then in charge of Spartak Moscow, we might have gone. Romantsev was a brilliant manager, who had just won the Russian championship three times in a row and was to win it five more times. He had taken Spartak to the semi-finals of the European Cup in 1991 and the last four of the Cup-Winners' Cup two years later.

In the first campaign they had beaten Real Madrid in the Bernabeu and in 1992 Spartak had thrashed Liverpool 6–2 on aggregate, winning both at the Luzhniki and at Anfield.

Romantsev had grown up on the Kola Peninsula in the far north of Russia and was very tough on discipline. He believed in promoting young footballers and was never without a cigarette in his hand. Some of his players at Spartak said they never asked for a transfer because they were afraid of going to his office to ask for one. I found him all right; neither hard nor soft, but then I had played under Lobanovsky and Ferguson.

Later, it was said Romantsev had problems with alcohol and was sacked by Spartak in 2003 after he accused the president, Andrei Chervichenko, of accepting $1.5m to throw the Russian Cup final against Rostov. Spartak won, 1–0.

Four of his players at Spartak Moscow had signed the letter complaining about Sadyrin but then they were persuaded to change their minds, probably because going to the World Cup would increase their chances of getting a transfer to the West.

Russia were not the only team at the 1994 World Cup who wanted a different manager. The Dutch wanted Johan Cruyff to manage them in the United States. Instead, they got Dick Advocaat, who was to manage me at Glasgow Rangers. Ruud Gullit walked out in protest before the tournament began.

I watched the 1994 World Cup on holiday in Marbella. Kuznetsov, Mikhailichenko and Romantsev also came to Spain and we played head tennis on the courts owned by Manuel Santana, who had won the Wimbledon championships in 1966.

Part of me wanted to be in America with the team but I told myself I had kept to my beliefs and not gone back on my word. I had little respect for those who had signed the letter and were then persuaded to be coached by Sadyrin.

To this day, I don't have much of a relationship with them. I have always thought that if someone betrays you once they will betray you again. If I see them, the words I will use will be 'hello' and 'goodbye'. I had much more respect for those who refused to sign the letter.

I sent the Russian team a fax wishing them well and I genuinely hoped they would have a good World Cup.

However, Russia were in a tough group with Brazil, who became world champions, and Sweden, who finished third. They lost their first two games and then beat Cameroon 6–1 in the last game in California. Oleg Salenko, who played for Dynamo Kiev, scored five times and his six goals in the tournament meant he shared the Golden Boot with Hristo Stoichkov of Bulgaria.

By the time we qualified for Euro 96, Romantsev had become the national manager but the draw gave us little chance of progressing. We found ourselves in the same group as Germany, who won the tournament, the Czech Republic, who came second, and Italy.

Our first game was against the Italians at Anfield and we needed a good start. After four minutes our goalkeeper, Stanislav Cherchesov, who is now manager of the Russian national team, cleared the ball straight to a blue shirt, the ball broke for Pierluigi Casiraghi and we were one down. Ilya Tsymbalar, who was one of Romant-sev's Spartak Moscow players, equalised in front of the Kop but Casiraghi scored again and we lost 2–1.

We were beaten 3–0 by the Germans at Old Trafford and our tournament was done. We did draw the final game 3–3 with the Czech Republic but I watched that game from the stands. Watching from the seats at Anfield was my last taste of tournament football. Russia did not qualify for the 1998 World Cup. By the time the 2002 World Cup came around my international career was over.

I never played in a World Cup but then nor did George Best or Ryan Giggs, two of the greatest footballers ever to wear the Manchester United shirt. Looking back, that is not bad company to find yourself in.

9
THE SAMOVAR

BUT FOR ERIC CANTONA WE WOULD HAVE WON A third successive league title. I do not mean that disrespectfully. But had Eric, under extreme provocation, not launched himself at a fan, Manchester United would have beaten Blackburn to the league title. Even without him for nearly four months we were only a point away.

On the pitch, Cantona's opponents tried everything they could to needle him. There would be sly kicks, a pulled shirt, an elbow. They wanted him to react and generally they would get what they wanted.

In January 1995 at Crystal Palace they hit the jackpot. I played in that game at Selhurst Park and watched him being led away after he had lashed out at Richard Shaw, who had needled him throughout the game. Then I watched a spectator, a young man, come running down the steps shouting at him. I thought he was half-drunk, maybe more than half-drunk.

Because I was by the touchline, I saw what happened next even though it took a long time for it to sink in. Cantona launched himself at the fan, two-footed, and sent him sprawling.

What was as remarkable about that kung fu kick was what happened in the dressing room after the match. I went in expecting the place to explode but nothing happened. Alex Ferguson went through the usual end-of-match debrief. He talked to Cantona about the build-up to the sending-off but not about the attack on the fan.

Cantona was treated differently to other members of that Manchester United side. Ferguson rarely shouted at him. I certainly never saw him get 'The Hairdryer'. Perhaps it was because Ferguson wanted to keep Cantona on his side or because he knew he did not react well to criticism. He may have recognised something of himself in Eric. I once heard him say to him in the dressing room, 'I was like you, Eric. I used to get lots of cards.' He did not shout much at Roy Keane, either.

Ferguson said afterwards that he only found out the full details of the incident once he got home. He said he thought a supporter had thrown something at Cantona but he must have known roughly what had happened. Somebody had to have told him.

We then had a shower and went to the bus for the flight back to Manchester. Nobody talked about one of the most bizarre things any of us had seen on a football pitch. Those of us who had actually seen what happened were still in a state of shock.

It was only the next day when we turned up for training at the

Cliff that the players felt able to talk about it. Then, the corridors were full of lawyers, people from the Professional Footballers' Association and the FA.

Looking back, it was probably just as well nobody went over to Cantona in the dressing room at Selhurst Park and asked why he had done it. There was an aura about him and he was not exactly an approachable man. If we had got into an argument with him about it, everything might have got out of control again.

It was like when a husband comes home drunk. If the wife demands to know where he's been, more often than not you'll get an argument that spirals out of control. If the wife just lets him sleep it off, then the next morning you can have a proper conversation.

We decided to let Eric sleep it off. Perhaps that is why Ferguson left him alone. Cantona had to settle it with himself before you could talk to him.

The FA banned him for nine months and at his criminal trial, after successfully appealing a two-week prison sentence, he was ordered to do community work with children, which I think he quite enjoyed.

When we arrived home from Crystal Palace we were one point behind Blackburn, although we had played two games more. We had beaten them 1–0 at Old Trafford the game before; Cantona had scored the goal.

Blackburn were a very impressive side who had bought very well under Kenny Dalglish. Alan Shearer, Chris Sutton, David Batty, Graeme Le Saux and Colin Hendry were the basis of a very good team but I think Manchester United were the better side. In the season Blackburn won the championship we beat them home and away.

The mark of a great side is how it responds to winning a title. When Manchester United won their first title after 26 years we could have relaxed and slipped down the table or we could have concentrated on the Champions League. Instead, we won it again and by a greater margin and we added the FA Cup. Blackburn very quickly faded away after 1995. That is the difference between a great club and a good side.

Every once in a while a club comes from out of the blue, surprises everyone and wins a title. Leeds did in 1992, Blackburn did it and Leicester did it in 2016. Rostov surprised everyone by coming second in the Russian Premier League. But it is not a success clubs like these tend to repeat.

Manchester United under Alex Ferguson was like a machine. It produced consistently. You can say the same about Bayern Munich, Barcelona or Real Madrid.

When Manchester United got into difficulties they would have years of experience of winning trophies to draw upon. Blackburn and Leicester did not have anything like that history to help them through.

Big clubs get hiccups. Manchester United have not won the Premier League since 2013. Everyone knew Ferguson was going to leave at some stage and everyone knew he would be difficult to replace. He had such a feel for the club. He knew which players would work for Manchester United and which would not.

His way of working was not primarily about spending money. He did not always get it right but he had been there so long and was such a dominant person that he influenced the whole structure of the club. His presence was in every girder of Old Trafford.

I was surprised Manchester United did not try to carry that on by replacing Ferguson with another man who knew every inch of the club. Ryan Giggs could not have done worse than David Moyes and Louis van Gaal and he might have done considerably better. The players would have followed Giggsy and so would the fans, and Ryan would have had an instinctive feeling for the kind of football Old Trafford wanted to see.

Many of that team went into management. I did and so did Bryan Robson, Mark Hughes, Paul Ince, Roy Keane and Steve Bruce. We followed Ferguson but I don't think any of us tried to copy him.

If we had, it would not have worked because we are different personalities and we do not have the same thought processes. When I went into management I was influenced by Ferguson but I also drew on my experiences with Claudio Ranieri and Valery Lobanovsky. But mostly I tried to be myself.

The season that saw me leave Manchester United was one of my best. Until I was injured in March, I don't think I have played better than I did in 1994/95. I scored fourteen times and, though I scored two more for Everton in the following season, overall I played better for United.

The opening months were all about the Champions League. This was the first time the Champions League looks like what it does now, first a group stage and then the knockout phase. We were the best team in England by a very long way but Manchester United did not get out of the group.

Keane once said that Cantona was not a player he could ever remember changing the course of a game in Europe in the way he did in the Premier League. If Roy was implying that Eric was part of the reason why Manchester United fared so badly in the Champions League, I cannot agree.

The biggest reason Manchester United did not do well in Europe in those years was nothing to do with Cantona but the UEFA rule that then stated you could only play three foreigners in your team.

Naturally, I was counted as a foreigner and so were Cantona and Peter Schmeichel, but Brian McClair was also 'foreign' because he was Scottish. There were too many 'foreigners' for Ferguson to squeeze into his team. It was a constant headache for him. He tried every kind of combination to fit the rule.

In the 1994/95 season Manchester United played three away games in the group stages of the Champions League. I was chosen for all three. In Istanbul, against Galatasaray, the other 'foreigners' were Schmeichel and Keane. In Barcelona they were Irwin and Keane and in Gothenburg Irwin and Cantona. We drew 0–0 in Turkey and were thrashed in Spain and Sweden.

The 4–0 defeat at the Nou Camp by Barcelona was a debacle in which I ended up playing left-midfield with Ryan Giggs going through the middle. Paul Ince kept going forward with Giggsy and left a huge space behind him that Barcelona poured into. The whole of the midfield kept opening up. Ferguson was furious with him but that was unfair because the whole team played badly.

As soon as UEFA allowed Manchester United to field their full team in the Champions League, they demonstrated what they were capable of.

To get back into the Champions League we had to win the Premier League. There was then no consolation prize for coming second or even fourth. The Champions League was then only for champions.

A few days after we were crushed by Barcelona I played my best game for United. I had never scored three goals in any game before but on 10 November 1994 I became the first United player in 34 years to score a hat-trick in the Manchester derby. We won 5–0; it was City's heaviest defeat to United in a century.

For the first time I felt able to do a television interview in English. It was one of the greatest moments of my career. Ferguson was thrilled. He'd been pleased with my performance against Newcastle when we'd won 2–0 the previous month but this time his smile was enormous. 'This doesn't happen every day, Andrei,' he grinned. From someone like Alex Ferguson this was as a big a compliment as you could get.

But at the time I felt blasé about it. I didn't go out and celebrate and because it was a Thursday night going out would have been difficult anyway. Yes, I had scored a hat-trick, yes, the team had won, but I was already thinking about the next game – a home game against Crystal Palace in which I would score again in a 3–0 win.

Perhaps my attitude was indicative of how well I was playing. When you are in form, you don't analyse it or reflect on it. Now, however, you look back and realise the scale and the drama of it.

But the team was becoming weighed down by injuries. By December we were missing Hughes, Schmeichel, Parker and Giggs. Keane played centre-half. In January, Cantona was banned. The pressure was on for those of us who were left. I suffered a double hernia. I was playing constantly for Manchester United and there was a heavy schedule of Euro 96 qualifiers with Russia and they took their toll.

Russia drew both games with Scotland. After the 1–1 draw at Hampden Park in November, Alex Ferguson drove me home from Glasgow. He joked that at least he would know what time I went to bed.

My last game for Manchester United was in April 1995, a 3–0 win over Arsenal at Old Trafford. Everyone seems to have a theory as to why I left. Some think it was pressure from the Russian mafia who wanted to make a financial killing from a big transfer. Others say it was because I had lost so much money in the city's casinos and that I needed the pay day I would get from a move. I heard these rumours when they first came out and they made me angry, although now they just make me smile.

If I were spending most evenings in a casino, it would have been pretty easy to find out – all casinos are equipped with cameras. And Ferguson would have known. He seemed to know everything his players got up to.

In 1995 people would stop me in the street and ask if I was in trouble with the Russian mafia. Even when I came back to Manchester 21 years later to write this book and met up with some United fans, their first words were: 'The mafia has come back.' I had to laugh.

I was not laughing then. I did not have a pistol pressed to the back of my head and I did not have a doorman at a casino asking me to pay my debts before I left. I did, however, have a terrible pain in my abdomen.

A hernia happens when part of your intestines pushes through your muscle wall. You can feel them protruding, sticking out of you. They don't suddenly appear; they develop over time. When I first came to Old Trafford, the physio was Jim McGregor, who was an excellent doctor but there was conflict between him and Ferguson and he left to set up his own clinic in Manchester.

He was replaced by a young doctor called Dave Fevre. He was just 34 years old when he joined from the Wigan rugby league club. I was feeling constant pain in my abdomen and told the doctor that

I couldn't sleep at night. It was slowing me down on the pitch, I couldn't move and I certainly couldn't play with the same freedom that I was used to.

Fevre asked if I was trying to get out of playing, if I was looking for an excuse to pull out of the squad. 'Why should I want to stop playing?' I asked him. 'I have scored fourteen goals and I am playing the best football of my life. Why should I not want to play for Manchester United?'

I went to Jim McGregor's home to see him and within three minutes of him opening his front door, he had diagnosed a double hernia. All he did was touch and feel my abdomen then he nodded his head and said, 'Double hernia.'

I went back to the club and sought out Dave Fevre. 'I have been examined by another doctor and he has told me I have a double hernia,' I informed him, though I didn't say I had been to see Jim. 'I am not trying to get out of playing and we need to resolve this. You need to treat me seriously.' The conversation got out of hand. Soon, we were having a big argument in his room.

The result was that I was authorised to have an operation but, although I trusted Jim McGregor's diagnosis, there were still some doubts running around my mind as I was taken to the clinic. Just for a moment, in the middle of the operation, I woke up and asked the surgeon, 'Do I really need the operation?' The answer was: 'Yes, you do.' Then I went back under the anaesthetic.

When I'd recovered I went over to Old Trafford, a few days before the final game of the season, for a meeting where everybody who mattered at the club was in the room. The chairman, Martin Edwards, was there, Ferguson was there, so was the secretary, Ken Ramsden. I went with my interpreter, George Scanlan, and my representative, Grigori Essaoulenko.

The anger had been building up inside me for days and in that room it just spilled out. I had the documents detailing the operation and why it needed to be done in my hand. 'You said I didn't need an operation, you said I was just trying to avoid playing. You didn't believe me and I want to leave the club.'

Ferguson was really strong. He said he had made a mistake in not believing I needed an operation and was willing to apologise. He said that, if necessary, he would be prepared to apologise in front of the whole team. I really admired him for that. He did not try to bury the issue or put the blame on someone else as he could easily have done.

Both Ferguson and Edwards told me how much they valued my contribution and how much they wanted me to stay at Manchester United. What I didn't know at the time was that Ferguson had already decided to sell Paul Ince to Inter Milan. Mark Hughes had already decided to leave Manchester United for Chelsea because he did not want to be the third-choice striker behind Cantona and Andy Cole, who United had signed from Newcastle for a record transfer fee. Ferguson and Edwards had a strong motivation to make sure I was not the third to go.

But Essaoulenko was determined that I should leave. There seemed to be a lot of pressure on him to do a deal. Had he been a stronger person, he could have said, 'Look, Manchester United want you to stay, they think you will be happy here. Honour your contract.'

But Essaoulenko was on a substantial commission to force through a transfer and his advice was not impartial. He would have been under a lot of pressure from Shakhtar Donetsk, who were entitled to at least £500,000 should Manchester United sell me. Some said the figure they eventually received was closer to £1.5m.

The club was run by Akhat Bragin, who a few months later would be killed by a bomb attack in his own stadium. It was a gang thing, a mafia thing. Essaoulenko told Ferguson and Edwards, 'He has to go, he has to leave.'

Looking back, it was a mistake on both sides. In 1994 I had signed a contract that would have kept me at Manchester United for five more years. It would have expired in the year the club won the Champions League. By then, UEFA had relaxed the foreigners rule and I would not have been under so much pressure to justify my place.

If Jim McGregor had still been the Manchester United doctor, he would have diagnosed the hernia correctly, I would have been treated and I wouldn't have been so full of pain and resentment towards the club. I wouldn't have been so ready to listen to Essaoulenko when he insinuated that Manchester United were treating me like a piece of meat by trying to force me to play when they knew I was badly hurt.

It was only later that I found out about the samovar. In Russia a samovar is a container that holds hot water to make tea. It is often beautifully decorated and has a handle and a tap. Only two people, Essaoulenko and Ferguson, know why my agent should stop the manager of Manchester United, ask to meet him at a hotel at the airport and give him a box containing a samovar which in turn contained £40,000 in cash.

I wasn't the only player Essaoulenko represented but I was the only player he represented at Old Trafford. But he didn't tell me he was going to do it or ask me what the best way to get hold of Ferguson was.

It was August 1994 and we were playing away at Nottingham Forest on Monday night. It had been a 1–1 draw at the City

Ground. I had scored the opening goal and Stan Collymore had equalised on the counter-attack.

Grigori had waited for the Manchester United team bus to get back from Nottingham and then arranged to see the manager. I don't know why they met at the airport but the next day Ferguson was flying to Sweden to watch Gothenburg play Sparta Prague. The winner would be one of our opponents in the Champions League.

Ferguson took the box home and counted the notes. He said he didn't know why he had been given the money. He said he thought it was so he would cooperate if another of Essaoulenko's players wanted a move to Manchester United. The money was put in the club safe and, eventually, returned to Grigori.

In the same season, George Graham, who was then manager of Arsenal, admitted that he had received a much bigger gift from Rune Hauge, an agent who had worked with Grigori. Graham banked the money and, when that was revealed, Arsenal sacked him. Ferguson returned his gift which was a very big decision – and a very good one.

At the time, I had no idea any of this was going on. I was at Rangers when Ferguson wrote about the incident in his autobiography. It was the first I knew about it. The one thing that does occur to me now is that Shakhtar Donetsk were entitled to another substantial payment if I played a certain number of games and this money may have been to ensure that this happened or to thank Ferguson once the number was reached.

It is a guess, probably the best guess I can give you, but only two men know what went on that night at Manchester airport, and only Grigori Essaoulenko really knows why he filled a samovar full of banknotes rather than water.

I was told I could leave. The summer of 1995 was the one in which Ferguson shocked Manchester United by allowing three senior members of his first team – me, Hughes and Ince – to go. He had decided to put his trust in the products of his youth team.

Those of us who were at Manchester United knew that this was not such a big gamble. We knew how strong the young footballers that Eric Harrison had produced were because we used to go and watch them play.

During the 1994/95 season Gary Neville had started playing regularly in the first team. He was behind me, a right-back while I was on the right wing, so I saw a lot of him. Paul Scholes was also breaking through while David Beckham and Nicky Butt were close to the first team. Everyone knew what Manchester United had coming.

The biggest beneficiary of my departure was David Beckham, who took my place on the right wing. He wasn't the only candidate, Ferguson had signed Karel Poborsky, who was part of the Czech Republic side that made the final of Euro 96, but Beckham was the one who made that position, my old position, his own.

He said in his autobiography that if I had stayed at Old Trafford his career would not have advanced as quickly or as spectacularly as it did. People now talk about Beckham as if he were only a celebrity, as if the only thing he did in his career was to marry Victoria and make commercials.

As a footballer, I would put him on the same level as Ryan Giggs and Paul Scholes. The difference was that, away from the game, Beckham enjoyed the limelight and the television cameras. If Giggs had wanted to, he could have become equally as big a celebrity as David Beckham.

What irritates me is that when people talk about Beckham they tend to focus on what he *didn't* do. He didn't make great runs with the ball, his pace was not electric. I prefer to judge sportsmen on what they do well, and with the ball at his feet, particularly a dead ball, Beckham could do extraordinary things. Sometimes, I regretted leaving Manchester United but I never felt jealous or envious of the men who replaced me. Nobody made me go.

It was a mistake for me to leave and perhaps I listened to the wrong people. If I moved from Manchester United, Grigori would make money and so would Shakhtar Donetsk. I would also benefit financially from a move – and Everton paid me the same salary as Manchester United – but I would have to re-establish myself at a new club.

I would be the one taking the risk and giving up a five-year contract at Manchester United. When you are at the centre of a transfer, you are always told things must be done immediately, now. You have to sign this piece of paper and then that one. Not only do you not have time to reflect, you are told you cannot have it.

My agent now is a Hungarian called Sandor Varga, who looks after Oleg Luzhny and Sergei Rebrov. I like to think that, had Sandor been my agent in 1995, he would have told me to go away for a few days, think it over with my family and ask if this was really what I wanted to do.

My relationship with Alex Ferguson is better than it was. Now that I have been a manager, I can begin to understand why he was so driven to succeed. Even in 1995, when he had won the Premier League twice, he still seemed under enormous pressure; much of it, I imagine, was self-induced.

He had been manager of Manchester United for five years before I joined and he was manager for eighteen years after I left. It is astonishing even to write it. Ferguson's achievements seem even greater when you look at the club's decline in the years after he retired.

I don't think it would even occur to him to regret the fact that he did not work abroad, that he did not manage a Bayern Munich or a Real Madrid. Can you think of a bigger club, a better club, than Manchester United?

He might have done well at Bayern Munich. Ferguson had no time for the tiki-taka, the passing for passing's sake that became such a feature of Spanish football. The style of play he insisted on at Old Trafford was all about precise passing of the ball to get it forward as quickly as you could. Bayern Munich's style was and still is very similar. They attack from the flanks with Ribery and Robben and have two centre-forwards in Lewandowski and Muller.

The job was too big for David Moyes but you could not blame him or any manager for wanting to sit where Ferguson had sat. The stagnation of Manchester United under Louis van Gaal came as no surprise.

When he became manager, I recorded an interview and said that Manchester United would not win the championship under Van Gaal. His style of slow, possession football was out of date and it was definitely not what Manchester United fans were used to.

The pressure on Jose Mourinho to drag Manchester United back to where they once were must weigh heavily but it will not compare to the kind of pressure on Ferguson when I came to a club that had not won the title for a quarter of a century.

The last time I saw him was in November 2016, 21 years after I'd left. He was much older, of course, more relaxed. Manchester United were playing Feyenoord and I went to Ferguson's box at Old

Trafford.

He was holding court, drinking wine, when he spotted me. Someone said, 'Now, there was a great player.'

'I know he was a great player,' Ferguson said. 'I paid £650,000 for him.'

I told him he should try Tuscan wine, the kind I drank when I played for Fiorentina. The subject of my departure came up as we talked and he said, 'It wasn't your fault you left United, it was Essaoulenko's.'

At the end of every season I played for Manchester United, just before I went home to Russia, Ferguson would say, 'Don't forget to bring me back a tin of caviar.' As we talked in his box, I pulled out something from my pocket – a tin of Beluga caviar.

A
KIND OF BLUE

'WHY ARE YOU LEAVING US? HOW MUCH MONEY did you gamble away? Is that why you needed the move?' I may have left Manchester United but I still lived in Manchester and whenever I went out there would be a fan who wanted to know why I had decided to go.

Mentally, it dragged me down. I felt low, depressed, worried. Now if a Manchester United supporter wonders why I left and mentions the gangsters I can laugh and say, 'Yes, I am mafia and you'd better be careful what you say next because I have a Kalashnikov under my coat.' But not then. Then there were no jokes.

I had told Manchester United I was leaving. They had accepted it. I was walking away from one of the biggest clubs in world football, a team I was very comfortable playing for. It was a team I was at home in, where I had friends. Now what?

You ask yourself so many questions when you leave a club. You wonder what the new manager will be like. When you are offered a new club you mentally go through their team sheet and ask yourself which of them you might get on with or which of them you might play well with. In the summer of 1995 there was a lot playing on my mind.

There were a lot of possibilities. Arsenal were interested and so, too, were Liverpool, but Alex Ferguson was adamant that I would not be doing any business with them because he said they were 'direct competitors'.

Middlesbrough was a serious option. They were managed by Bryan Robson. He really wanted me to come and the idea of playing for my old captain was very appealing. Bryan had looked after me when I was at Manchester United and he would look after me at Middlesbrough.

There were problems. The main one was that Middlesbrough and Manchester United could not agree a fee. The other was where Middlesbrough was. It was a long way north and, if I moved, I would have to move my family.

Everton was another option. My interpreter, George Scanlan, was a big Everton fan and told me plenty of stories about the club – and that was a major influence on me. The other big draw was that, if I moved to Everton, I could stay where I was.

It was George who made the phone call to the Everton manager, Joe Royle, to tell him I might be going to Middlesbrough. I knew him as the manager who had taken Oldham to the FA Cup semi-finals and who had just won the FA Cup for Everton by beating Manchester United in the final, a game I did not play in because of the hernia operation, although I travelled with the squad to Wembley.

Joe came to my house and told me not to go to Middlesbrough: 'Why would you want to go there? It's like Chernobyl.' He knew that part of me would have wanted to play for Bryan Robson but he knew, too, that I wanted to stay in the north-west. He was flattering about my play, saying that my absence from the FA Cup final had given Everton a substantial advantage and he had used that in his team talk at Wembley.

There were delays in completing the deal. There was a dispute as to who should pay the money to Shakhtar Donetsk, who claimed they were owed £1.5m. Manchester United thought Everton should pay. Everton thought it was United's debt.

In the end Manchester United paid but they did not transfer the money they owed Shakhtar Donetsk until quite late, which meant I missed Everton's Charity Shield win over Blackburn at Wembley and the first two games of the season. I also missed the UEFA registration for the Cup Winners' Cup.

When doing business with clubs from the former Soviet Union you have to look beneath the surface. There is a proverbial story of how the chairman of Dynamo Kiev is bid £5m for a player and that night he goes to the casino and loses £2m. The next day the fee rises to £7m.

Andrei Yarmolenko could and should have gone from Kiev to Everton in the summer of 2016 but the price kept changing. Everton were quoted £20m for the forward and then it became £25m and, eventually, the deal didn't happen. I joked to myself that the directors of Dynamo Kiev must be losing an awful lot of money in the casinos.

I played in most of the other games and scored sixteen goals. In that season at Goodison, I changed my style of play. I became much more of a number ten or an attacking midfielder and much less of a winger. I loved my football, I loved the crowd.

If I had to pick the years when I played my best football, it would be between 1994 and 1996, one season at Manchester United, the other at Everton. I would have scored more than fourteen goals in my last season at Old Trafford but for the hernia injury, and I began the season late at Goodison Park.

What I began to do was cut inside because my opponent would expect me to go outside to deliver a cross for Duncan Ferguson. I scored a lot of goals by doing that and it was something I decided to do for myself. It wasn't one of Joe Royle's ideas.

I can remember one of the first times I did it. At Goodison Park the dugouts are very close to the pitch and the crowd and I could hear a lot of what was being said. One Everton fan told me that when I cut inside Royle was yelling, 'Keep wide, Andrei, keep wide. I said keep wide, keep wide. Cross it, cross it. Oh, great goal, Andrei.' Soon, he saw the method of what I was doing.

Everton finished sixth, which was our best finish since 1988. I got on well with Joe. There was a really good dynamic between him and his assistant, Willie Donachie, which put me in mind of the one between Alex Ferguson and Brian Kidd at Manchester United.

At United, Ferguson was the emotional one, he would motivate us, fire us up for the next game so that we played beyond our abilities, but it was Kiddo who gave it all structure in the training sessions. Sometimes, when Kiddo went abroad to Spain or Italy to study training at another club, Ferguson would stride over to take training and we all pretended to boo him. We loved Brian. They were a good team, one balanced out the other.

Joe was a good person, a kind man. He would always try to get us laughing and joking in the dressing room but Donachie was really tough, really strict. At the training ground at Bellefield he would try to squeeze the very most out of you. If you didn't perform, he would get really angry.

When he was at Newcastle, he had to resign after they alleged he hit one of his players after an under-21 game at Sunderland. You can't hit players these days but I am certain Donachie would only have done it because he cared so much about his teams.

Players aren't supposed to answer back, they are supposed to train. You can go to the trainer's office after the session and make your point but not on the pitch in front of everyone else. That's what I learned from Willie Donachie. When I was a manager, if any player wanted to argue with me, I would send them straight to the dressing room.

I knew plenty about Everton before I came to Goodison Park. Gary Lineker, Andy Gray, Howard Kendall and Alan Ball were big names wherever you lived. If there were gaps in my knowledge, George Scanlan made sure they were filled in.

It was a smaller club than Manchester United but it had plenty of history and very passionate supporters. The one difference with United was that at Everton, even if the team wasn't winning, the fans would still be very loud and very emotional. I enjoyed being in Liverpool. The people were far more straightforward and far more ready to talk to you than they are in London. The city was much easier to get to know than London or even Manchester.

Whenever I come back to Merseyside I am always amazed how many people want photographs or an autograph or just want to talk football. For some reason, I seem to get a bigger reaction when I go to Liverpool than when I go to Manchester, which is strange when you think that I played four years for Manchester United and eighteen months for Everton.

When David Moyes said, 'The people on the streets of Liverpool support Everton,' I think he was right. I appreciated the fact that the fans who came to Goodison, far more than Old Trafford or even Anfield, were local. To me, that mattered. It gave them an extra edge.

Joe Royle was building up a very good side. Duncan Ferguson, Anders Limpar, Nicky Barmby and Graham Stuart were pretty formidable footballers. Dave Watson and Neville Southall were a link to the club's glorious past that George never tired of telling me about. To me, Everton were not a world-class side like Manchester United but they were a good team in a quiet, unobtrusive way.

It was a very good dressing room. Everyone was very straight-forward with each other and there didn't seem to be the kind of politicking that you get at some clubs.

Despite all this we did not start at all well. By the time we played Blackburn on 5 November, we had won two league games – and none at all since August – and been knocked out of the Cup Winners' Cup by Feyenoord. Everton were in seventeenth place.

In September, I had come face to face with my old Manchester United team-mates at Goodison Park. It was a match I had been anticipating from the very start of the season. I lasted five minutes. Lee Sharpe had scored after three and I was trying to take the ball past him when he bundled me over. When I sat up, my shoulder was dislocated.

Everton lost that game 3–2 but you could see that Manchester United were changing. David Beckham provided the cross for Sharpe's first goal and hit the bar with a free kick. He was twenty

With my agent Grigory Essaoulenko at the 1991 League Cup final, prior to my Manchester United move. United lost 1-0 to Sheffield Wednesday **(Colorsport)**

Posing for a photo with Sir Alex and fellow new signings, Paul Parker and Peter Schmeichel. **(Mirrorpix)**

In the wall during the 1991 European Super Cup clash with Red Star Belgrade. Neil Webb and Paul Ince on my left, Mark Hughes on my right. **(Offside)**

Running down the wing in the League Cup final against Nottingham Forest, 1992. A 1-0 win secured my first silverware for United. **(Colorsport)**

Representing the CIS (the provisional national team of the Soviet Union) at Euro 1992 against Scotland. We lost the game 3-0, and it was my last tournament before I started representing Russia. **(Colorsport)**

Playing against Denmark in a friendly just after they had been crowned champions at Euro 1992. It was the last ever game the CIS played. **(Offside)**

With legendary goalkeeper Peter Schmeichel in 1992. We have both arrived at Old Trafford in 1991. **(Getty)**

With my interpreter George Scanlan, who helped me settle in my early days in England. **(Getty)**

Seeing red in the 3-1 League Cup final defeat to Aston Villa in 1994. I handled the ball in the 90th minute with our side 2-1 down. (**Colorsport**)

Battling with Robbie Fowler of Liverpool. This fixture, especially in the 90s, was the biggest game in English football. (**Offside**)

Celebrating with King Eric after he scores in the Manchester Derby, April 1994. We were on our way to another league title. **(Offside)**

With Lee Sharpe during the homecoming parade around Manchester, following the 4-0 FA Cup Final win against Chelsea. **(Getty)**

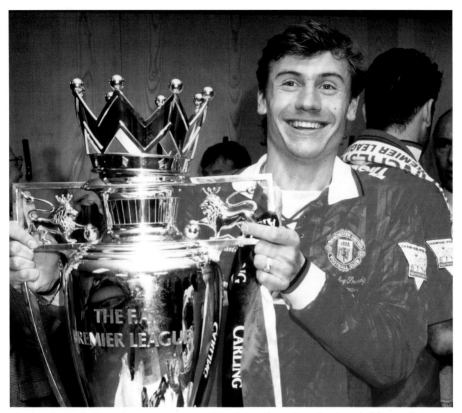

The second time I had won the Premier League trophy with Manchester United, at the end of the 1993/94 season. **(Getty)**

Wheeling away in celebration after scoring my third goal in the 5-0 victory over Manchester City in November 1994. It was my only hat-trick for the club. **(Getty)**

Rounding off proceedings during a 3-0 win over Arsenal in March 1995. We would just miss out on the Premier League to Blackburn Rovers during that campaign. **(Getty)**

Celebrating with Duncan Ferguson after scoring in the 2-1 victory at Highbury in January 1996. **(Colorsport)**

Taking on Paolo Maldini during our 2-1 defeat to Italy at Euro 96. **(Getty)**

Skipping past Newcastle's John Beresford during a 2-0 win, August 1996. **(Getty)**

Back in action for Russia in a World Cup qualifier against Bulgaria in Sofia, September 1997. **(Getty)**

On the ball during my first season at Fiorentina, February 1997. **(Getty)**

Taking on the Inter Milan back line at the San Siro. Diego Simeone is in the background. **(Getty)**

Welcomed to Scotland by Hearts midfielder Gary Locke, August 1998. **(Getty)**

Celebrating my first European goal for Rangers, against PAOK Salonika, August 1998. **(Getty)**

With teammate Sergio Porrini after the 4-0 win over Aberdeen in the 2000 Scottish Cup Final. **(Getty)**

Pressuring Galatasaray's Hakan Unsal during a Champions League clash in October 2000. **(Getty)**

A young Steven Gerrard tackles me during my loan spell at Manchester City in January 2001. **(Getty)**

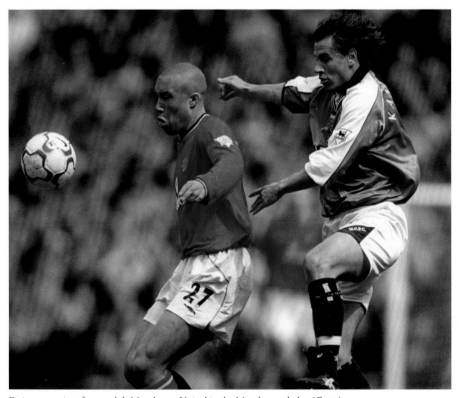
Facing up against former club Manchester United in the Manchester derby. **(Getty)**

Facing up against another one of my old clubs, this time Everton, in my only Premier League appearance for Southampton **(Colorsport)**

Part of a wall while playing for Saturn Moscow Oblast on my return to Russia, June 2005. **(Getty)**

In action for Krylia Sovetov against Rubin Kazan in the Russian Premier League, March 2006. **(Getty)**

My son Andrei Jr playing rugby. He played to a very high level before going to university. **(Andrei Kanchelskis Jr)**

I was particularly proud to see my old club Manchester United lift the Champions League trophy in my home city of Moscow in 2008. **(Getty)**

My daughter Eva.
She studies Politics and
Religion at university.
(Andrei Kanchelskis Jr)

Myself, Andrei
and my good friend
Dave Cockram at
USM Finch Farm, 2016
(Andrei Kanchelskis Jr)

With my former Fiorentina manager Claudio Ranieri, who of course won the Premier League with Leicester City (Andrei Kanchelskis Jr)

Reunited with my first manager in England, Sir Alex Ferguson, last year. I made sure to bring him a tin of Black Russian Caviar. (Andrei Kanchelskis Jr)

years old. Nicky Butt, Paul Scholes and Gary Neville were all play-ing. These were Ferguson's kids, the men who would provide the backbone of the new Manchester United.

It was mid-October when I was fit enough to play again, in a 1–1 draw at Bolton, where Paul Rideout scored a late equaliser. But gradually Everton began playing better and better. We lost 3–1 to Newcastle at the start of October but we lost only once more at Goodison Park in the rest of the season.

If we had started like we finished, Everton would have ended up in the top three or four. For me the highlight would always be 18 November, when I scored twice to win the Merseyside derby at Anfield.

They were the first goals I had scored for Everton and they were in the biggest match of all. Everton were to win only one more game at Anfield in all the years that followed. The key to that victory was the sheer aggression with which we started the game, something which Liverpool weren't ready for and couldn't handle. We were desperate to beat them. We could and should have overcome Liver-pool by a wider margin than 2–1.

For the first goal I passed to Paul Rideout with a flick of my boot and ran towards the Kop for the return. His cross was perfect and I headed it in off the post from somewhere near the penalty spot.

The second was from a diagonal pass from Anders Limpar. Of all the players at Everton, I got on best with Anders, who was my room-mate on away trips. I hit the shot hard with my right foot and it was too powerful for David James in the Liverpool goal. Anfield went quiet; all you could hear were the Everton fans screaming at the other end of the stadium. Two goals. At Anfield. Scored in front of the Kop. You dream of these things.

I loved playing against Liverpool. They weren't the first goals I had scored against them. The season before, I'd scored for Manchester United against Liverpool at Old Trafford, the opening goal in a 2–0 win. The reaction then had been impressive but this was extraordinary.

In April, Everton faced them again, this time in terrible, heavy rain at Goodison Park. Again I scored. It was a long ball that James missed but John Ebbrell somehow pulled it back from the by-line. He struck the crossbar and I managed to drive it in. We would have won that game, too, but Robbie Fowler equalised with a few minutes remaining. In my time at Everton we did not lose a Merseyside derby.

Duncan Ferguson had been signed by Everton the year before I arrived. He was young and very aggressive. He got into all sorts of fights but, when you are young, you make mistakes because you don't know how to react.

People were wary of Duncan. He had been to prison, he had a really explosive temper, but in football sometimes you find your club and when Duncan came to Everton from Glasgow Rangers he had found his club. The supporters regarded him as a legend.

He reminded me of Mark Hughes. Off the pitch he was a very quiet, very reserved kind of guy but on it he became a beast. He never talked to me about his hobby of pigeon racing and, if he had, I don't know what I would have made of it. I know pigeons were used to deliver messages during the world wars but I don't think any Russian would comprehend the idea that you could make a sport out of it.

For a three o'clock kick-off at Goodison Park we were expected to arrive at 1.25 p.m. and as soon as he arrived in the dressing room Ferguson would run himself a bath and read the matchday programme in it.

One of the other things some Everton players used to do was put their boots in the bath before kick-off. I had never seen this done before and when I asked why I was told it was 'to soften them'. I said, 'But won't they just get heavy?'

When I returned to Everton for pre-season after Euro 96, there was plenty of optimism. We had finished sixth and had finished strongly. This was the first season in which England would send two clubs to the Champions League. Blackburn had won the title in 1995, why not Everton in 1997?

It might sound fantasy now but we had signed Gary Speed from Leeds, who was just the kind of goalscoring midfielder that Everton needed. I had had a few tussles with him when Manchester United played Leeds and I'd been impressed. We began the season by beating Newcastle, who had finished second in the Premier League the previous season and were considered the most exciting team in England.

We won 2–0 at Goodison Park. Speed almost scored early on from one of my crosses and, after David Unsworth had scored a penalty, Speed scored the second on his debut. He was 26, born in the same year as me; he had won the title with Leeds and had come to Everton, the club he supported as a boy. It must have been one of his very great days.

Of course, I heard about what happened to him. That he hanged himself. I only played with Gary for six, seven months but I remember a fine, intelligent footballer who seemed to be in the middle of a great career. When people talk about footballers, they always say, 'But you have so much money, really, what pressure can there be?' The money doesn't change you; it doesn't alter who you are. The money is a mask. It's there for you to hide behind.

The next game was at Old Trafford on a Wednesday night. At the interval, we were 2–0 up on Manchester United and playing beautifully. Duncan Ferguson took my pass with his back to goal, turned and shot Everton into the lead. Six minutes later, he headed Andy Hinchcliffe's cross past Peter Schmeichel.

With 21 minutes to go, Johan Cruyff's son, Jordi, headed home and then David Unsworth deflected a cross past Neville Southall for the equaliser. Manchester United had been fortunate to draw and for much of the game Everton had been the better side.

It had been a match between two high-quality teams and there was talk in the Everton dressing room that maybe we could really challenge for the title. In the event, Manchester United would finish the season as champions. Everton would finish two points away from relegation.

The third fixture was at Tottenham and, again, the way the game went gave us little inkling of the crash to come. We drew 0–0 but Everton should have won easily. I had a long-range shot very well saved by Ian Walker. Craig Short missed a free header and Duncan Ferguson might have scored right at the end. We had five points from three matches but we should have had nine.

Alexei Mikhailichenko was living in London at the time and I had asked Joe Royle if I could stay down after the match. We had a day off on the Sunday so there was no problem.

Alexei planned to meet me at White Hart Lane but the parking around the stadium was so bad we had to walk about a mile and a half to get to his car. We passed a pub full of Tottenham supporters and one of them called me over. He said something abusive to me and when I answered him back he threw a full pint of beer in my face.

I lunged at him. All I wanted to do was punch this thug. In my ear I could hear Mikhailichenko shouting, 'Andrei, get out. If you don't, we're going to be beaten to a pulp.'

There were about 200 Tottenham supporters in the pub and most of them seemed to be coming very aggressively towards us. There were shouts of 'Russian bastards'. People have told me that my pace was the key to understanding my career. It was certainly the key to escaping from that pub.

We did not win another game for six weeks and we were knocked out of the League Cup at York. We were sixteenth in the table and Liverpool were top. My form had started to fall away.

It is hard to explain why you suddenly lose your touch. My two worst seasons in Britain were in 1992/93 and 1996/97 – immediately after a European Championship. One of my best came in 1994/95 after I had boycotted the World Cup. Russia failed to qualify for France 98 and I won the treble with Glasgow Rangers the following season. It seems too much of a coincidence.

Perhaps, because my game was based so much on pace and power, it could not stand eleven months of action. What nagged away at me was how badly Russia had done in Euro 96. I was 27, the age when you start asking yourself if you have reached your peak and the rest of career will be a slide from the top.

I was too young, really, for the European Championship in Sweden and in any case we had all the baggage from the break-up of the Soviet Union to cope with as a team. I had missed the 1994 World Cup through what I still believe was an act of principle.

If I were to shine at a major international tournament, then the European Championship in England – staged in a country where I was living and playing my football – should have been it. Instead, it had been a deep, lasting disappointment. I hadn't had a proper holiday to let those frustrations melt away and I had taken them into the new season, where they had stayed. When it came to January and the ultimatum as to whether I should stay at Everton or go to Fiorentina, this feeling, that I needed a fresh start in a new environment, was probably the decisive one.

On 28 September, we won our first league game since the opening day, beating Sheffield Wednesday 2–0. It was my first goal of what was proving a very different second season at Everton.

Nevertheless, we began playing better. Everton won four of the next six games, including a 7–1 victory over Southampton. I scored two and Gary Speed three. On the pitch, it appeared for a moment that things were righting themselves. However, off it, there was more and more uncertainty spreading through the club.

What I heard was that, early in the season, Joe Royle met the club chairman, Peter Johnson, to be told there would be much less money for player transfers. At the same time, I was told there were several Italian clubs would be interested in me, including AC Milan and Fiorentina.

While Arsenal, Manchester United, Liverpool and Newcastle seemed to have limitless budgets, Everton's appeared to be contracting rapidly. There was talk that Everton had to leave Goodison Park if they were going to compete.

When I returned to Goodison twenty years after I left Everton, it looked exactly the same as it did when I played there and the newspapers in Liverpool were still writing about plans for Everton's new stadium.

What really struck me about Manchester United was how determined they were to expand the capacity of Old Trafford. Just after the Cantona affair, we lost at Everton. That game at Goodison was watched by 40,000, which was slightly less than the capacity of Old Trafford, which in 1995 was 43,000.

Now every Manchester United home game is watched by 75,000 and Everton actually have a slightly reduced capacity from what they had in the 1990s. They do at least have a new training ground, which is sponsored by a company owned by the Arsenal investor, Alisher Usmanov. He and the Everton owner, Farhad Moshiri, are very close. The football world is very small and news travels around it very quickly. It was no surprise that the two of them linked up.

Even when I was working for Usmanov in Russia ten years ago, I could see how well the two of them worked and perhaps they are the best bet for Everton's new stadium, although when it comes I will miss the sound of Goodison Park.

Then one day, in January 1997, not long after one of our worst performances, an FA Cup defeat by Bradford, I got a phone call from George Scanlan telling me not to go home but to stay in Liverpool.

At about six o'clock George and I went to a meeting at Goodison Park. Johnson wasn't there but all the rest of the Everton directors were. We were told Everton had reached an agreement with Fiorentina to sell me for £8m.

They explained that they had more or less accepted the offer in principle but it was up to me whether I went to Italy. If I wanted to stay at Everton, I could.

To tell you how advanced the discussions were before I was called over to Goodison, I began the meeting with the directors at six o'clock and at ten a private jet belonging to the president of Fiorentina was ready at Liverpool airport to take me to Florence for the medical.

I had two hours to make a decision. Fiorentina's sporting director was at Goodison. I talked to him and I phoned Inna, who was in Moscow. 'It is your career, you are the player, you decide,' was her advice. One of the things we had to consider was young Andrei, who was still in pre-school.

On one side I liked Everton and I especially liked their fans. They had always supported me. I was told that Joe Royle wanted me to stay and I knew the players wanted me to stay. I think the directors wanted the £8m. In 1997, £8m was a lot of money.

Joe Royle was under a lot of stress, you could see it etched into his face. He knew, more than any player or supporter, just what the financial situation was. He was an honest man who could not easily hide his feelings.

As a player, he had won the championship with Everton in 1970 and there were some who thought he might just win it as a manager. But it was January now and all those hopes had been smashed. He was replaced two months after I left.

There were tensions within the squad. Neville Southall had been Everton's greatest goalkeeper but he was 38 now. Royle thought him a fading force and wanted to replace him. Neville thought that he was not being given an opportunity to prove himself; the opportunity his record with Everton demanded.

There were by then plenty of injuries but Everton did not have the depth of squad to cope. Royle had wanted to bring in a goalkeeper and a centre-forward, Mark Schwarzer and Tore Andre Flo. One went to Middlesbrough, the other to Chelsea.

I had a contract and there were plenty of people who thought I should have honoured it. However, if I stayed, what sort of club would I be committing myself to? Royle had been regularly complaining to the press that he wanted to bring more players to Everton to make the club into the force it looked like being last season but that he was being prevented from doing so by the chairman.

At Manchester United I had been at a club who used every season to bring in new players to build on what they had already achieved. They had an academy that had been set up to guarantee the future. This was very different: there was no long-term policy, no strategy and, we were told, no money. The optimism of the summer had been replaced by a hand-to-mouth existence.

I was not immune from the criticism. I had not been playing well, I was struggling with an ankle injury, and some fans and a lot of the press seemed to think that if I had scored sixteen goals in my first season at Goodison Park, I should be scoring sixteen in the second.

There was a lot of stress and a lot of pressure. When Inna and I discussed our future I told her that I thought the club would sell me but that they would wait until the summer. Suddenly, there was a decision to make and hours in which to make it.

I had known for some time that Serie A was an option but I had no idea that abstract conversations would suddenly become serious. What had happened was that the Fiorentina board had heard Milan might be interested in taking me to the San Siro and they had decided to act quickly.

When I boarded the jet, one insurmountable problem struck me. I was a Russian citizen and when we landed in Florence, I would be asked for my visa. I didn't have one. I didn't even have a passport. I would be immediately and humiliatingly deported. But when the president's plane landed, everything was waved away. Nobody asked to see my passport. I signed the contract the next day.

9
THE BOTTICELLI MURDERS

WHEN I ARRIVED IN ITALY, IT WAS PROBABLY THE
centre of the football world. AC Milan had won the Champions
League in 1994 and Juventus were the reigning European champions. Between 1992 and 1998 an Italian club had reached seven
successive European Cup finals.

I didn't speak Italian and we had to move our family from Cheshire
to Florence but this was an arena I badly wanted to test myself in.
They found us a home not far from the Piazzale Michelangelo,
from where you can see the city of Florence spread out before you.

Behind it was a winding road that went up the hills above the city
and that's where we lived. It was spectacular and no journalist ever
asked me if I had any connections to the Russian mafia or whether
I spent every night in a casino.

They should have asked because I very quickly came face to face with the real mafia. We lived in a two-storey duplex in an apartment block. Once, soon after I arrived in Florence, I found the place sealed off by the police.

They did not understand English and at this stage I spoke barely a word of Italian so I had no idea what was going on. I had to phone one of the women at the club who spoke English so she could try to explain it to me.

When the police broke into the flat they found a body and a Botticelli painting that had been torn from its frame and had blood poured over it. That was a signal that the man had been killed – battered to death with a baseball bat – because of a blood feud. I was told later that eighty years before exactly the same thing had happened; a body had been found next to a blood-covered Botticelli. Welcome to Italy.

Fiorentina were managed by Claudio Ranieri and the president was a man called Vittorio Cecchi Gori. He had inherited the club from his father, Mario, who was a film producer and friend of Silvio Berlusconi.

Mario and Vittorio would produce films together. They worked with Federico Fellini and Adriano Celentano, who was one of Italy's most popular singers, who became an actor and director. Their biggest hit was a film called *Il Postino*, which was nominated for five Oscars. They were royalty.

Just before we played AC Milan, Vittorio addressed the squad and told them that, if we won, he would give everyone a Rolex watch. We didn't get the watch. We didn't beat Milan. Cecchi Gori then told us that if we beat Roma we would get the watch. We didn't beat Roma. The Rolexes were not offered up again.

He was a very generous man, an open soul. He had a celebrity marriage to Rita Rusic, who was eighteen years his junior. Rusic was a model from Croatia who had made her name as a teenager in the Milan fashion world. When they married Rusic became involved in Cecchi Gori's films and made records. Vittorio became a senator. They had two kids, a lot of money and a very high profile.

The death of his father Mario in 1993 had been a big blow but it was when his mother died that Cecchi Gori went completely off the rails. She had been able to keep Vittorio in check but, once she was gone, he did what he liked.

He lost a fortune buying the television rights to Serie A and then he split up from Rita. The divorce cost him millions and, as he went down, Fiorentina went down with him.

Eventually, after Fiorentina had gone bankrupt and were liquidated, Cecchi Gori was arrested in bed with his mistress, a bag of cocaine and several million dollars. It was like Al Pacino in *Scarface*. He was later convicted of embezzling £26m from Fiorentina's accounts in an attempt to prop up the rest of his collapsing business empire. He was saved by Silvio Berlusconi, because of his friendship with Cecchi Gori's father. Berlusconi was the man who had closed Mario's coffin at his funeral.

That was all in the future for Fiorentina. In January 1997 they were the holders of the Coppa Italia, had beaten Milan in the Italian Super Cup and they boasted one of the great strikers in world football – Gabriel Batistuta, whom Diego Maradona reckoned the greatest centre-forward of his lifetime.

However, the problem Fiorentina had was that, Batistuta apart, they were a good side rather than a great one.

In 1995, Batistuta had been Serie A's leading goalscorer with 26 goals but Fiorentina had finished only tenth. They won the Coppa Italia the following year and finished fourth – but they were still fourteen points adrift of Milan. When I arrived, they had a good first XI but Claudio Ranieri had very little cover on the bench if anyone got injured.

On the training ground, Stefan Schwarz, who had come to Fiorentina after a season at Arsenal, translated for me. I found myself speaking Italian more quickly and fluently than I had ever learned English.

At Manchester United and Everton, George Scanlan went everywhere with me to translate. He probably made things too easy for me because without him I would probably have learned English a lot quicker and spoken it better.

When you signed for an Italian club they expected you to learn Italian immediately. It took me six months to speak it well. I fell in love with Italy. When you travelled around Italy, you realised that it was not one country but a series of regions, each with its own traditions and culture.

Tuscany, where I lived, was famous for its meat dishes and red wine. In Naples it would be seafood and white wine. When you went to Turin, you learned that the wine there was stronger than anywhere else.

There could have been few more beautiful cities in which to live than Florence. If I were on my own after training or on days off, I would go to the galleries: the Uffizi, which housed the real Botticellis, and the Accademia, where Michelangelo's statue of David was the centrepiece.

Florence is a small city, very easy to get to know. Sometimes, we would drive out into the mountains and sit out on a restaurant terrace where you could see the old city below you. The club arranged for the players to have 20 per cent discounts in the Gucci store in the city centre, but we rarely went because it was always so full of tourists.

Sometimes, if you did go shopping, you'd find yourself in a boutique and the owner would come over and say, 'If you score against Juventus at the weekend, you can take your pick of anything in the shop. Anything you want, it's yours, but please score.'

If the players went out in the city itself, it would be to a little restaurant tucked away in one of the side streets. It was a wonderful life – until the weekend came, when you absolutely had to perform.

Not only were the fans expectant, they could also be violent. Hooliganism was once thought to be a British problem and when you saw the Leicester fans in Madrid shouting about Gibraltar, before their Champions League quarter-final with Atletico, perhaps it still is. As we saw in the European Championships in Marseilles, it is a Russian problem but it has also been an Italian problem.

For all the talk of its sophistication, I was amazed to see supporters in Serie A separated by what looked like bullet-proof shields and with moats to stop them invading the pitch. The final of the Coppa Italia between Napoli and Fiorentina in 2014 was delayed for 45 minutes because of violence that saw three Napoli fans shot.

The Stadio San Paolo, where Napoli play, was one of the more testing experiences of my career. When there was a game on, people who lived anywhere near the stadium tended to say indoors. If they ventured outside, they risked having their bags snatched by thieves riding Vespas.

Once, when I was being driven through Naples, the driver had his windows down and his arm hanging out of the car as he drove.

A scooter sped by and his watch was gone. If you were an opposition fan going to the San Paolo, you risked being stabbed.

There has always been a dark side to the Italian game. Toto Schillaci, the hero of the Italian World Cup, came from the streets of Palermo which were run by the mafia. His career in Serie A was mainly spent in Turin and Milan, and whenever things went wrong he was greeted by taunts of 'mafioso' or 'tyre thief' because his brother had been convicted of stealing tyres. His first wife was accused of being implicated in the collapse of a jewellery business.

Carlo Ancelotti tells the story that when he was assistant manager of the Italian national side he and Arrigo Sacchi were invited to a dinner in New York. It was a mafia dinner and everyone wanted them to invite Schillaci. Ancelotti told Sacchi they should leave while they still could.

There was never any evidence that Schillaci – a very humble man, who found being a national hero difficult to deal with – ever took an order from the mafia. They 'adopted' him because he was Sicilian. That was the other side of Italian football.

However, the rhythm of the game was much more like I was used to in the Soviet Union. There, we would stay the night before a game at the training ground, which had its own accommodation built into it. In Italy they would always go to a hotel the day before a match and they would sometimes have two training sessions a day. Your diet and your weight were monitored in a way it never was at Old Trafford or Goodison Park. I can't ever remember being weighed in England.

It was easier to go from the Premier League to Serie A than it was to move from Italy to England as Andriy Shevchenko did. Not only was there a similarity in the way teams in Italy and the Soviet Union prepared, there was more of a similarity in the style of play.

Marcello Lippi and Fabio Capello had, after all, come to Kiev to study Valery Lobanovsky's methods and occasionally I would see something and think to myself that I knew where that move came from.

There was no pre-match meal of chicken and beans. The club had its own team of chefs who served chicken with pasta and salad about eleven o'clock for a 3pm kick-off. Pasta is much more quickly absorbed into the system than baked beans. There would be plates of Parma ham and the evening before the game they would serve you a glass of red wine.

At Manchester United, Paul Ince would keep a small bottle of brandy beneath his towel and just before the team was due to go into the tunnel and on to the pitch, he would take a little swig, just to steady himself for the game ahead.

When Cecchi Gori brought Batistuta to Florence from Boca Juniors in 1991, money was not an issue. He was the team captain and the idol for everyone who passed through the gates of the Artemio Franchi stadium. When Fiorentina were relegated in 1993, he stayed with the team and won them promotion rather than accept transfer offers from the likes of Manchester United.

The fans paid for a bronze statue of Batistuta to be built outside the stadium, holding a corner flag, which was one of his celebrations whenever he scored, and when he went to a restaurant they would never allow him to pay. He would offer up bundles of lire after a meal but they were always waved away. He was loved, he was adored. He was like Maradona in Naples. A god.

But he was also a very simple, straightforward man who reminded me very much of Bryan Robson, especially in that he would always be giving you little pieces of advice. He was the polar opposite of Eric Cantona, a man who craved his own company. If he saw you,

Batistuta would seek you out for a chat.

He was devoted to his wife, Irina, whom he'd met when they were sixteen and fifteen respectively. He was a family man, who was comfortable to be around. He was not particularly interested in the trappings of football and although all footballers, especially centre-forwards, have egos, Batistuta appeared to have less than most.

He told me that he always looked back on his childhood for inspiration. His family were from the port area of Buenos Aires, a place of meat-packing plants and oil refineries. His father worked in an abattoir and, although they moved, they were still very poor. Gabriel would make money by roaming the streets and collecting discarded bottles which he would take back to the shop for the deposit. He used to remind himself of that when the season got rough.

His mood in the dressing room was nearly always good but he was also a natural-born captain, who knew how to motivate his team. He was one of those who, if they were not involved in a game of football, would not be particularly interested in watching. His sport now is polo.

After his first season, when he scored fourteen goals, he never scored fewer than nineteen for Fiorentina, which in a league as defensive as Serie A is an astonishing achievement. His greatness lay not just in the quality of the goals he scored but in how consistent he was.

When Fiorentina won the Coppa Italia in 1996, Batistuta scored in every round except the first. They won the semi-final against Inter Milan 4–1 on aggregate and Batistuta scored all four. When they won the trophy, Cecchi Gori presented every member of the team with an Audi.

By the end of his career, Batistuta's legs had been so wrecked by football, he could barely walk. The cartilage in his knees had gone, his ankles were agony. He once pleaded with a doctor to amputate his legs just to relieve the pain. The doctor refused. Gabriel Batistuta is the greatest forward I have ever played alongside.

He gave everything to Fiorentina but he could never win the Scudetto there and, eventually, he left for Roma. They paid £23m for him, which was a record for a player in his thirties. Roma beat Parma on the final day of the season to win the title.

Batistuta scored in that game, although Fiorentina meant so much to him that when they gave him the freedom of the city of Florence he apologised for going to Rome. I was glad he did; he would never have won the Scudetto had he stayed.

It was not just in the pre-match meal that the differences between English and Italian football showed themselves. Tactically, the average Italian defender was far more astute than his English counterpart. I found English defenders to be physically very strong but very weak when it came to knowing where to position themselves. In Serie A you were given no room, no space to play in, while the referees would constantly interfere. I found my early games against Maldini, Baresi and Cannavaro very difficult. They did tell me that when I found my feet in Italy it was difficult to play against me, which I thought a very high compliment.

However, I had to completely adapt my game, which showed in the number of goals I scored. Admittedly, I was injured a lot, but in Serie A I scored just twice.

The Italian game may have been technically better but the Premier League had a dynamic that they never approached in Italy. When I think back on Serie A to the time when it was the best league in the world, I recall the style of Maldini and the brilliance of Batistuta but I also remember the diving, the feigning of injuries and the referee's whistle shrilling every few minutes.

Serie A was a great experience but, in truth, I didn't enjoy watching it. I missed the aggression of the English game.

The resurgence of Juventus, who were the best team in Europe in the 2016/17 season, is a demonstration of what Italian football should be about. In the decade since AC Milan beat Liverpool in Athens to win the Champions League, Italian football had found itself in a ditch. It was no longer the richest league in the world. It was eclipsed by Spain and England and even Germany.

For footballers of my generation, Italy was always where you earned a lot of lire and it should have stayed that way. One of the big reasons for the decline of Italian football was Italy's decision to join the euro. Their economy was not ready for it and an economic decline set in that affected everything, including football. Now, looking at the way Juventus reached the Champions League final in 2017, beating Barcelona and a brilliant Monaco side, Italian football has once more reached the peaks.

I liked Ranieri. He was a very sophisticated manager who spent a lot of time talking to me about the way he would like me to play. He was also very good when it came to giving you bad news.

If he was going to leave you out of the starting line-up, Ranieri would sit you down and explain that the match that was coming up was not so important; he really wanted you fit and ready for the one that followed it. That was the match that really mattered.

You would leave his office thinking what a good conversation you'd had with him. Only then did it sink in that he had just dropped you. He was always polite and would never raise his voice in the dressing room.

When I arrived in January the club was in trouble. Fiorentina did not win away from the Artemio Franchi for the rest of the season and eventually finished ninth. Juventus, the Juventus of Del Piero, of Zidane, of Edgar Davids, of Lippi, won the title that year and they would do it again the next.

We reached the semi-finals of the Cup Winners' Cup but were beaten by Barcelona, who were then managed by Bobby Robson. As I had at Everton, I had arrived too late to be registered for the competition. Ranieri was sacked at the end of the season.

He deserved better and I was pleased for him when he won the Premier League with Leicester. It was one of the greatest of all sporting stories, but when Leicester sacked him I was not as shocked as everyone else. When you have been in the game any length of time, you realise that it is essentially cruel. Even the greatest stories can end messily. It is, I am sorry to say, the life of a coach.

I have been both a player and a manager and it is always easier to play. When the final whistle blows a footballer goes home and the match and its result doesn't tend to stay with him very long. Only if he has been at the centre of a dreadful error does it tend to stay with him throughout the week.

If you are a manager, every game stays with you. You go home, you put on the DVD and you analyse every mistake, you ask yourself if you could have done something better. You worry about what the president might be thinking. As a coach, the game never leaves you.

The one thing you have to have as a manager is effective communication with the president. Alex Ferguson and Martin Edwards had that relationship when I was at Manchester United.

Too often, and this is especially true of football in Russia, the president will interfere and think that because he has been successful in business he knows football – that his money gives him the right to interfere. Cecchi Gori interfered all the time. The man was crazy, nuts.

He had paid £8m to Everton for me without once asking Ranieri if he thought it was a good idea or whether I would fit into his plans. The only conversation Ranieri had about me was Cecchi Gori telling him: 'We need to buy Kanchelskis. I am sending my plane to Liverpool.'

Ranieri was replaced by Alberto Malesani. He had no sort of career as a professional footballer but he had taken Chievo from Serie C and had almost promoted them to Serie A when Cecchi Gori hired him. He was said to have been so obsessed with coaching techniques that he spent his honeymoon in Barcelona just so he could watch Johan Cruyff coach.

I enjoyed working with Malesani and we started the season well with a 3–2 win at Udinese, which was our first away win in eight months, and followed it by beating Bari.

In the third game, against Inter Milan at the San Siro, Taribo West flew into a two-footed tackle and broke my ankle. I was taken straight from the pitch to the hospital and was out for two and a half months.

It meant I missed the serious part of Russia's attempt to qualify for the 1998 World Cup. Our group was a straight contest between Bulgaria, who had finished fourth in the United States World Cup, and ourselves.

We would play each other in the final two games, matches which because of Taribo West's tackle I would miss. We won the second 4–2 in the Luzhniki but the fact that we lost the first 1–0 in Sofia had made it irrelevant. Bulgaria would go to France as group winners. We would have to play off – against Italy.

I was not ready and I should not have played but the manager, Boris Ignatiev, told me I had to. I was one of the leaders of the team and I was playing in Serie A. Even my presence in the squad would mean something.

The first leg, which ended in a 1–1 draw, was in the Dynamo Stadium in Moscow in late October. The weather was atrocious, the stakes were enormous and after half an hour I collided with the Italian goalkeeper, Gianluca Pagliuca, and broke my kneecap.

I don't know whether it was because the knee was numbed by the shock or whether it was because it was so very cold but I played on for another quarter of an hour. Pagliuca had been taken off on a stretcher straight away to be replaced by the nineteen-year-old Gianluigi Buffon, who was to become one of football's greatest goalkeepers.

As soon as I went into the warmth of the dressing room, I felt this excruciating, crippling pain. I spent an agonising night in Moscow and then I was flown straight back to Italy for treatment.

The return game was seventeen days later. I was in Florence with Plaster of Paris encasing my leg when I got a call from Ignatiev. He wanted to know if I could come down to Naples to join the team.

I assumed he wanted me to be with the squad to boost morale and because I could still give them practical advice on how some members of the Italian team might perform. But no, Ignatiev wondered if I was fit enough to play.

'I've got a broken kneecap,' I told him. 'My leg's in plaster.'

'Are you sure you are really hurt?' Ignatiev replied. 'It might be that nothing is broken and that the Italian doctors have tricked you so you can't play against them in Naples.'

'I will come down and show you the X-rays.'

I didn't play against Italy in the San Paolo. I didn't play for another four and a half months. We lost 1–0 to a Pierluigi Casiraghi goal and with that defeat went my last chance of a World Cup. My time with Fiorentina was also running out.

Fiorentina finished fifth in 1998, which was enough to secure European football but not enough to keep Malesani his job. The Fiorentina directors were terrified that Batistuta would leave if the club didn't start challenging for the Scudetto.

They hired Giovanni Trapattoni, who had just finished a stint at Bayern Munich. He signed a forward, Edmundo, who had just won the Brazilian league with Vasco da Gama and a defender, Tomas Repka, from Sparta Prague.

Trapattoni told me straight away that because of the number of foreigners in his squad I could expect very little game time. Batistuta, naturally, would always play. Edmundo and Repka would nearly always play. I should look for another club. I appreciated his honesty.

As it turned out, Edmundo didn't always play. He was called 'The Animal' for his behaviour on and off the pitch. By February 1999 it looked like the plan to stake everything on winning the Scudetto was going according to plan. Fiorentina were top of Serie A.

The trouble was Batistuta had picked up a serious injury and nobody could get hold of Edmundo. He had flown back to Rio de Janeiro for the Carnival. Fiorentina had just drawn 0–0 with Milan and were preparing to face Udinese, a game they lost 1–0. When the news channels screened coverage of the Carnival, the team gathered round a television set trying to find Edmundo in the crowd. They were utterly shocked to the core.

He stayed drinking and partying for three days in Rio before flying back to Italy. Cecchi Gori loved Edmundo so much that there was no question of actually punishing him for it. But the club still paid a price. After Edmundo's disappearance, Fiorentina won only three games in three months and lost the final of the Coppa Italia to Parma. They were expensive drinks.

10
BATTLES WITH THE LITTLE GENERAL

THERE WERE PLENTY OF CHOICES IN FRONT OF ME
in the summer of 1998. I could stay in Florence but, as Giovanni
Trapattoni told me, there would be very few games. The only way I
would get in the side was if one of my team-mates were injured or if
Fiorentina were failing or if Trapattoni were to be sacked. You can't
really plan your career on the basis that others will fail or get hurt.

Alberto Malesani, who had made way for Trapattoni at Fiorentina, had gone to Parma and there was a real prospect of me joining
him. It would have been a very good season. Parma won the Coppa
Italia, beating Fiorentina in the final, and they also won the UEFA
Cup.

Fiorentina were disqualified from the competition after one of
their fans threw an explosive flare at a linesman during a match

with Grasshoppers Zurich. One of the teams Parma knocked out on the way to winning the trophy was the one I ended up joining – Glasgow Rangers.

Metz, who had only missed out on the French championship on goal difference and could offer Champions League football, were interested but everything was decided by the size of the transfer fee. Rangers offered £5.5m and neither of the other clubs could match them. It was then the highest fee ever paid to bring a footballer to Scotland.

The other big plus was that, if I moved to Scotland, I and my family would be eligible for a British passport. I would have dual citizenship and that meant a lot.

Also, we still had our house in Cheshire. We would have to rent in Glasgow but it gave us somewhere to go while we organised the move to Rangers. There were two people I asked for advice before deciding to go. One of them was Alexei Mikhailichenko and the other was a woman called Valya Valentina, who had helped Alexei with his move to Rangers from Sampdoria in 1991.

Alexei had retired a couple of years before and was living in London but he flew up to discuss the move with me. He and Valya both said the same thing. Rangers were a good club with good fans and Russian people were treated well in Glasgow – Alexei was Ukrainian but in Scotland they didn't differentiate. He told me that it was the best club he had ever worked with.

I found Glasgow a similar kind of city to Liverpool and I liked the people in the same way. After four years of Alex Ferguson, I could cope with the Scottish accent.

The most impressive person at the club was its chairman, David Murray. This was a man who had lost both legs in a car crash when he was 25 and had gone on to build up one of the wealthiest businesses in Scotland. Under him, Glasgow Rangers became the biggest-spending club in Britain and one of the biggest transfer dealers in Europe.

There were similarities between what I found at Ibrox and the club I had left behind in Florence. Both had new managers: Dick Advocaat had replaced Walter Smith, who had gone to Everton. Both were determined to spend what it took to win the league. Fiorentina's motive was to keep Gabriel Batistuta, while Rangers had just failed to record a tenth successive Scottish league title. Murray was adamant there would not be a second successive failure. There was also another similarity although nobody in either city could possibly have been aware of it. Both Fiorentina and Glasgow Rangers would go bankrupt and be liquidated.

The obvious difference between Serie A and the Scottish Premier League was that in Scotland there was not the layer of top, international-class footballers that there was in Italy. On the other hand, the desire to win was the same in both countries and in Scotland the commitment was greater. If you were 2–0 down with a few minutes remaining, nobody threw their hands up and waited for the final whistle. You played and you fought until the last minute.

I wouldn't say that Scottish football was just Glasgow football. My first league game was in Edinburgh where we lost to Hearts. Trips to Aberdeen were hard. Everyone raised their games against the Glasgow teams. If they beat you, the game would be immediately released as a DVD in the club shops, the goalscorer would be treated like a legend. Everyone would talk about it.

I loved the atmosphere of the Glasgow derby. Some footballers don't enjoy the big occasion, they shy away from it. Eyal Berkovic, who Celtic bought from West Ham when John Barnes was managing the club, was someone who never seemed to fancy a Glasgow derby. Berkovic was so intent on pulling out of a tackle that at Rangers we nicknamed him 'The Grasshopper'. He was a skilful player but in those kinds of games the crowds valued fight more than delicate displays of skill.

For me, the pressure was something to embrace. I had endured being on the wing against Galatasaray in the Ali Sami Yen and the barrage of coins and cigarette lighters that came with it. By that standard, Celtic Park was not that intimidating. Nobody threw things at you.

Yes, there would be abuse shouted at you but when you were playing, you were so wrapped up in your thoughts, so cocooned in the game, that you barely ever heard it or were even aware of it. When you were warming up you would catch the remarks, but once the game started your senses developed a kind of tunnel vision.

The derby with Celtic was everything. They started talking about that game weeks before. You'd pick up a paper – any paper – and the only subject worth writing about seemed to be Rangers v Celtic. You'd turn on the television and it would be there in front of you. We would always stay in a hotel the night before a match to prepare for it – which Rangers then never did for home games.

For the 1999 Scottish Cup final against Celtic, which was at Hampden Park, less than four miles away from Ibrox, we checked into a hotel three days before the game.

No derby I have played in, not Manchester or Merseyside, ever had the attention that the Glasgow derby received. You wondered if anything else was happening in Scotland.

I lived outside the city on an estate that had quite a few Rangers players. You quickly learned that when you went into the city there were some bars and restaurants that you went to and some that you avoided. Once I was driving through Glasgow, got lost and ended up in Parkhead right next to Celtic's ground. Suddenly I was aware of people on the streets pointing, shouting and swearing at me. It was lucky I was in a car.

My first football encounter with Celtic was rather more painful. It was on a September evening at Ibrox, I was running down the wing when Stephane Mahe launched himself into a high tackle. I fell backwards, thrust out my arms to break the fall and fractured one of them. I knew straight away it was broken. This was the fourth serious injury I'd suffered in two and a half years at three different clubs. The routine was becoming familiar: going to the training ground but not training. Being alone in the gym with just a physiotherapist and waiting for someone to collect you when everyone else has gone home.

I was fit to play in the return game in November, which in a way was even more painful. Celtic, who were having a dreadful season and were in the middle of an attempted boardroom takeover, thrashed us 5–1. It was Rangers' worst defeat in a Glasgow derby for 32 years. It kicked off at three o'clock on a Saturday and was one of the last derbies not to be televised live, which was just as well for our half of the city.

On 2 May 1999 Rangers won the title at Parkhead. It was the first time in their history they had won the championship at Celtic. I wasn't part of Advocaat's team but the atmosphere was even more intense than usual for a Glasgow derby.

Stephane Mahe, who had injured me in the first derby of the season in September, was sent off in tears during the first half. Celtic finished the game with nine men, Rangers with ten. The referee, Hugh Dallas, was hit by a coin thrown from the stands. Rangers won 3–0 and Neil McCann, who was a Catholic, scored two of the goals. At the end the Rangers players went into a huddle on the centre circle to celebrate, which enraged those Celtic supporters who were still in the ground. Eventually, the stewards told the team to go to the dressing room for their own safety. When Dallas returned home, he found his windows had been smashed.

Celtic Park was slightly bigger than Ibrox and there they sang the most beautiful songs. I found Celtic's songs inspiring rather than intimidating. One of the things that marked out the Glasgow derby for me was the singing. Both sets of fans sang loudly and passionately and they sang to the end. The only place I have been where the singing was anything like that was the Kop at Anfield. They would sing even if they were losing.

In January 2016, I went to Old Trafford to watch Manchester United lose to Southampton and the mood was quiet and sullen. The crowd didn't try to lift their team, but at Ibrox I think they would have done.

Rangers won the treble in Scotland in my first season. We beat St Johnstone in the League Cup final; we won the Premier League by six points; and we beat Celtic in the Scottish Cup final.

We did not parade the trophies through the streets of Glasgow as Manchester United had paraded the Double through the streets of their city. After winning the league the players were taken back to Ibrox, via a very long detour, where a huge crowd had gathered. Had we wanted to take an open-topped bus through the streets of Glasgow, we would have needed hard hats and protective clothing had the route gone anywhere near Celtic's side of the city.

There was plenty to celebrate in my time at Rangers. In March 2000, I was played through by Giovanni van Bronckhorst and became the first man to score in a Manchester, a Merseyside and a

Glasgow derby. Celtic were managed by Kenny Dalglish that afternoon and they were beaten 4–0. I had a hand in three of the goals and the defeat left Celtic fifteen points adrift.

They were probably beaten before the game began. Celtic had appointed John Barnes as their manager, had just sacked him after a dreadful run, and Dalglish had come in to try to help the club end the season with a bit of dignity. Celtic still tried to play it like a derby; there were plenty of tackles and yellow cards but psychologically they could not cope. We won the league by 21 points.

When we won the title, which was Rangers' eleventh in twelve years, David Murray paid for the whole squad to go to Marbella for five or six days to celebrate. Everything was paid for. I'd been to Marbella a few times and knew quite a few good restaurants in the town. I told the lads where they could find the best places for steaks or fresh fish. When I mentioned it to the Scottish contingent they said no, they'd be fine with a McDonald's.

Shortly after I joined Fiorentina in January 1997, I was exploring the city when my son, Andrei, who would have just turned four, asked to go to McDonald's. I took him there, ordered something for him but nothing for myself. The next day I was contacted by the club's technical director who said, 'Let me tell you: no Fiorentina player goes to McDonald's – ever.' Someone had seen me and reported back to the club.

The Rangers captain, Barry Ferguson, who was a really good guy and a very fine player, would go to McDonald's three times a week for a McChicken sandwich. In Marbella, once they had finished with McDonald's, they all went to Lineker's Bar and, once there, they did not leave. For them, lager and a Big Mac was the key to Spanish cuisine.

In Glasgow, we used to go to a Chinese restaurant, particularly after we'd won. One evening some official cars drew up outside and a man, dressed in a suit, came in to ask if they had a table for Prince Charles. He was on his way back from an official function in Glasgow and wanted something to eat.

The official was told that the restaurant was fully booked.

'But it's Prince Charles.'

'Well,' said the owner, indicating the room, 'which of these people do you want me to ask to leave?'

Prince Charles and his entourage drove away to seek out a more pliable restaurant owner.

Rangers won five trophies in my first two years at Ibrox. Judged by that, Dick Advocaat, who people nicknamed 'The Little General' because of his size, seems a very good manager.

However, I didn't enjoy playing under him and found him a very arrogant man who smiled very little. He was not in the same class as Alex Ferguson, Claudio Ranieri or Valery Lobanovsky, although he probably imagined he was.

Advocaat treated his players as if they were at a public school or a military academy. When we finished training we would go to Ibrox for lunch, which would be served at exactly two o'clock. Not five past, not five to, but at 2pm precisely. Latecomers were fined.

You would only be allowed to start eating when Advocaat came into the room and wished everyone 'bon appétit' or whatever. You could not leave the dining room to go home until everyone had finished. I hadn't had to obey those kinds of instructions since I was in the army and when I signed for Rangers I was approaching thirty years of age.

The food in the Rangers canteen wasn't actually that good and some of the foreign players would spend the time nursing cups of tea until Advocaat told them they could leave. They would then search out a restaurant.

When we went out he liked everyone to be wearing the same V-necked sweater. If you turned up in a polo-necked sweater, he would fine you. He also had a thing about white socks. You had to turn up in white socks. Brown or black were not allowed. Coloured boots were definitely out. I had a contract with Asics that required me to wear white boots. This made Advocaat extremely agitated. 'You can't play in white boots,' he would tell me.

To him, football was all about these kinds of petty details. When the Rangers captain, Lorenzo Amoruso, was spotted walking through the team hotel with his shirt outside his shorts, Advocaat gave him a lecture about the importance of tucking it in. The team was in Norway on a pre-season tour.

You wondered how Advocaat would ever have coped with someone like Eric Cantona.

There was no comparison between Advocaat and Ferguson when it came to man-management. I remember when Manchester United started the first season of the Premier League badly. Ferguson told the squad we all going off to a hotel to play golf. I think it was Mottram Hall. We arrived in the evening, checked in and Ferguson told us to meet in the bar in fifteen minutes. Then he went over to the barman and said, 'You've got the evening off.'

Ferguson went behind the bar and began serving his players anything they wanted to drink – beer, wine, whatever. Soon everyone had a drink in his hand and the whole team were just talking to each other, chatting, laughing.

It was a great atmosphere and it was exactly what Ferguson wanted because he knew the key to team spirit is communication.

Coming from the Soviet Union I was astonished to see the man who ran one of the biggest clubs in Europe mucking in behind the bar without any airs or graces.

The next day the squad went off to the golf course – I didn't because I don't play golf. But it was a great couple of days that re-energised the squad. We returned to Old Trafford and put together a run of victories and by May we had won the league. Ferguson, perhaps appropriately, was at the same hotel, playing golf, when he was told Oldham had beaten Aston Villa and Manchester United were champions.

Advocaat would never have had the imagination to have done that. And, if he had tried it, it would not have worked because there were too many cliques at Glasgow Rangers, mainly because there had been so many imports from Holland.

I thought his favouritism towards the Dutch players at Ibrox was blatant and it scarred my attitude towards him. I trained hard but, whether rightly or wrongly, I thought that when he picked me for some games Advocaat wanted me to fail.

Tactically, he was nowhere near as impressive as Ferguson. When I arrived at Ibrox, Rangers were as dominant in the Scottish Premier League as Manchester United had been in the Premier League when I'd left Old Trafford.

However, Ferguson's tactics were nearly always aggressive. He would always back Manchester United to outscore the opposition. Advocaat was generally far more cautious. When Rangers attacked, the instructions were generally to leave five in defence or well behind the ball.

What gave Advocaat the edge over Celtic were the huge financial resources that David Murray made available to him. He paid a Scottish record transfer fee for me. He spent only slightly less – £4.5m – to bring Arthur Numan from PSV Eindhoven. He bought Ronald de Boer from Barcelona. He paid £5m to Feyenoord for Giovanni van Bronckhorst. Another £3.75m to AZ Alkmaar brought Fernando Ricksen to Ibrox. For what was a moderate league, that was a lot of money.

Their goalkeeper, the German Stefan Klos, who had won the Champions League with Borussia Dortmund, had a salary of £4.5m, which made him one of the highest-paid players in world football. You cannot spend £80m with the kind of revenue streams that Rangers had at the turn of the century.

The rot that led to the downfall of Glasgow Rangers began here. There were some good games but, given how much Murray had invested in the squad, there was not much of a return. The money that Advocaat was allowed to spend was directly responsible for the club's bankruptcy.

Advocaat behaved like a man who had just come across a windfall and went shopping buying on impulse rather than thinking about what he needed. Players would be bought and then Advocaat would think about how they might be fitted into his team, when it should have been the other way round.

Some of the money was completely wasted. The summer I arrived from Fiorentina, Rangers spent £2m buying the Atletico Madrid defender, Daniel Prodan. He had played for Romania in the 1994 World Cup but the club did not even submit Prodan to a medical examination which would have shown he had a serious knee injury.

It was so serious that Prodan never played for Rangers and was released three years later. He was a good guy who died much too soon from a heart attack at the age of 44.

What Rangers lacked was togetherness. They had a very good team but there were too many cliques for it ever to have had much spirit. Celtic had far fewer resources but it seemed to me they had rather more spirit.

Advocaat was a man very motivated by money – spending it and earning it. In 2007 he took Zenit St Petersburg to the Russian Premier League. It was the first time a club from outside Moscow had won it since Alania Vladikavkaz in 1995 and the first time Zenit had won a title in 23 years.

However, Advocaat was given huge financial backing from Gazprom, the company that produces a sixth of the world's natural gas. It is so powerful that President Putin chose its chairman, Dmitri Medvedev, to succeed him as the country's leader. In the run-up to Zenit's championship-winning season, Advocaat spent nearly £40m on players like Pavel Pogrebnyak and Anatoly Timoschuk. He had not lost his habit of buying Dutch, bringing Fernando Ricksen from Rangers, where he had fallen out of favour with the new manager, Paul Le Guen.

The following season he won the UEFA Cup, beating Rangers, of all teams, in the final in Manchester, but he was sacked because he had signed a contract to manage Belgium at the end of the Russian season and Zenit's results were falling away badly.

To say you are going to manage somewhere else and try to carry on in your current job is always a mistake and too often one motivated by money. Advocaat was paid £1.3m to manage Belgium and then, when he had failed to take them to the World Cup in South Africa, he broke his contract and went to manage Russia for an enormous salary.

They made it to the European Championship but, like Rangers in the Champions League, Russia did not get out of their group.

Advocaat already had a job lined up with PSV Eindhoven.

The money spent caused other, more immediate, problems at Ibrox. At one time, if you included the management, Rangers had eight Dutchmen, which was far too many. At the same time Advocaat was managing in Glasgow, Louis van Gaal was doing much the same at Barcelona and being accused of bringing a Dutch mafia to the Nou Camp.

There was a Dutch clique at Rangers who hung out together. I was friends with Stefan Klos and Billy Dodds. The one Dutchman I really got on with was Arthur Numan, but the rest kept their own company.

Cliques at any club destroy an atmosphere and damage potential. Like Rangers, Van Gaal's Barcelona won domestic trophies but did not perform in the Champions League.

It was that kind of pro-Dutch atmosphere that brought my career at Ibrox to an end. In November 2000 I got into a fight on the training pitch with Fernando Ricksen. Advocaat was Dutch, Ricksen was Dutch, and I was the one who was blamed for starting it. I hadn't: Ricksen had simply scythed me down and I had reacted, but that didn't seem to matter.

Usually, whenever two players square up to each other on the training ground, the manager or coach will send them both off. Now, the only person Advocaat told to go to the changing rooms was me. He had shown everyone on the pitch whose side he was on.

Advocaat called me into his office and told me that I would be playing with the reserves at Aberdeen. My attitude about playing with the reserves was the same at Rangers as it had been at Manchester United. 'I signed a contract to play in the first team not the reserves,' I told him. Advocaat told me he needed numbers to make up the reserve team.

'What size boots do you take?' I asked him.

'Forty-two.'

'Well in that case go and get a pair of size forty-two boots and make up the numbers yourself.'

Outside Ibrox, the coach had arrived to take the reserves to Aberdeen and by the bus Advocaat was waiting just to make sure I was on it. I wasn't anywhere near Ibrox. I was at home, having dinner. An hour later a letter arrived, hand-delivered, informing me I had been fined a month's wages.

It was then that Advocaat's attitude to me changed. From that moment on, he was looking for a way to get me out of Glasgow Rangers.

During my time at Ibrox, Rangers accumulated the best footballers in Scotland but what they never really had was a team, and they suffered for that when Martin O'Neill took over at Celtic. O'Neill built a team and in his first season, Celtic won the treble and then retained the league title in 2002. By then, Advocaat was no longer manager.

He had resigned in December 2001, when Rangers were twelve points behind Celtic. He did not, however, leave the club. They created a position for him of 'general manager' and they kept paying him until Advocaat found a new job as manager of the Dutch national team. David Murray had proved himself once more to be a very generous employer.

11
AGENT ORANGE

MY FIRST ENCOUNTER WITH GLASGOW RANGERS came in an auditorium at Dynamo Kiev's training ground.

Valery Lobanovsky had called the squad together because he wanted to show them a videotape. When he put it in, Lobanovsky turned to us and said, 'This is how to defend.'

The match was Rangers versus Celtic. Lobanovsky said it proved you can defend with power and passion, not just by taking up the perfect position. He also pointed out that in a Glasgow derby nobody feigned injury, nobody rolled over pretending to be hurt, they just played hard. We were frankly shocked by the sheer aggression on the pitch.

There was a lot of respect for Rangers in Kiev. Two years before, in 1987, they had beaten a very good Dynamo side in the first round of the European Cup. I wasn't in the Kiev first team but I knew a lot of the players – Bessonov, Baltacha, Kuznetsov and Mikhailichenko. Kiev had won the first leg but lost the tie at Ibrox amid a ferocious atmosphere. Graeme Souness was the player-manager, Ally McCoist had scored the winner. I knew the kind of club I would be joining.

Ten years later, I was playing in the fixture that had so intrigued Lobanovsky and what I learned is that you can never duck out of a tackle, you can never fail to commit because the fans will not let you. Had Rangers kept hold of Gennaro Gattuso, they would have had a footballer who would have revelled in those matches.

Gattuso was only a teenager when he came to Glasgow from Italy and just twenty when he returned to Serie A. At Milan he linked up with Andrea Pirlo and Andriy Shevchenko and played in three Champions League finals.

Perhaps if Dick Advocaat had not played him as a right-back and then sold him a couple of months after I arrived at the club, he might have ensured Rangers did better in Europe.

Gattuso had a similar attitude to Roy Keane – winning to him was everything – but I thought Keane the better player. He could attack as well as defend and he scored goals, which Gattuso, generally, did not.

If you judged a season only on the results, my first season at Rangers was astonishing. We did not just win back the championship from Celtic, we won every domestic trophy. In terms of what we won, it was better than Manchester United in 1993/94.

The beginning gave you no indication of what was to come. I had not arrived in Scotland in time for the first match, which was a UEFA Cup qualifier against the Irish club, Shelbourne. Because of fears of sectarian violence, they had played the away leg not in Dublin but at Tranmere Rovers. Rangers found themselves three goals down before turning the match on its head to win 5–3.

On 2 August 1998 I made my debut for Rangers. It was not especially auspicious. We were at Tynecastle, facing Hearts. I was brought on at half-time when we were 2–1 down but the scoreline did not change. Celtic, meanwhile, had thrashed Dunfermline 5–0. However, although Celtic may have been champions, they were not a happy club. Wim Jansen, one of the few people in football Johan Cruyff said was worth listening to, had resigned. Rangers were spending a lot of money and Celtic, by comparison, were not. With the quality of signings David Murray was financing at Ibrox, Rangers had the strength of a top-six Premier League team.

I knew their captain, Lorenzo Amoruso. He had been at Fiorentina when I arrived from Everton and he left for Scotland at the end of my first season in Serie A. Lorenzo was typically Italian. He was passionate about the game and extremely emotional. He did not often lose his temper in the dressing room but when he did it was wise to keep your distance.

When Advocaat arrived at Rangers, he wanted to install Arthur Numan, whom he had brought with him from PSV Eindhoven, as captain. Numan, who was one of the Dutch contingent I really liked, was an intelligent man who knew that it would create divisions if a newcomer was made captain straight away. Advocaat offered it to Amoruso, who was a Catholic. It was a brave decision.

The partnership ended in November 2000. Rangers were playing Monaco at Ibrox in a game they had to win to stay in the Champions League. They were winning 2–1 when Amoruso made a mistake that cost them an equaliser and Advocaat immediately stripped him of the captaincy. Amoruso never forgave Advocaat.

He accused his manager of trying to destroy him.

There was a reason behind Advocaat's anger. One of the main reasons for Murray's hiring of him had been to improve Rangers' performances in Europe. They had been Scottish champions nine times in a row but only once, in 1992/93 when they just failed to beat Marseilles for a place in the final, did they really meet the expectations of their fans. The following season they were knocked out in the first round by Levski Sofia.

Advocaat had been brought in because Rangers imagined a foreign manager would do better in Europe. Advocaat had won the Eredivisie with Eindhoven and taken them to second place in a difficult Champions League group behind Dynamo Kiev but ahead of Newcastle and Barcelona.

One of the reasons why Advocaat failed was because there were so many new players arriving at Ibrox that it would take time for them to gel into a team. However, I think that Rangers, like Celtic, faced their own problems when they played in Europe. Outside Glasgow, Edinburgh and Aberdeen, the standard of Scottish football is mediocre. The step up to the Champions League or even the Europa League is often enormous. It is the same in Russian football now.

My first start was in the UEFA Cup second qualifying round against PAOK Salonika, then managed by Oleg Blokhin, who had been part of the Dynamo Kiev side beaten by Rangers in 1987. They had their midfielder, Triantaphyllos Machiaridis, sent off after eight minutes of the first leg but Salonika still harried us until ten minutes after half-time when I scored on my debut, heading home a deep cross from Rod Wallace, who scored the second.

In my first season Rangers reached the third round of the UEFA Cup, where we faced Parma, the club I could have joined in the summer. We drew the first leg 1–1 at Ibrox and lost the second 3–1. I played in the first match but not the second; I went with the squad to Italy but I was too ill to play.

Parma's stadium, the Ennio Tardini, is not much to look at but on the pitch my old manager, Alberto Malesani, had a fabulous team to direct – Buffon, Cannavaro, Thuram, Dino Baggio, Crespo and Veron. They would win the trophy in the Luzhniki, crushing Marseilles 3–0 in the final.

Rangers actually took the lead in the second leg. Jorg Albertz, another player who found life with Advocaat difficult, scored from the edge of the area when Roberto Sensini passed straight to him.

It may have been played in Italy – in the early afternoon as I recall – but it was not much of a game for Rangers' Italian contingent. Sergio Porrini was sent off while Amoruso handled the ball when he was under no pressure to give away the penalty for Parma's third goal.

Under Advocaat, Rangers played reasonably well in the Champions League but there was never a big, standout victory. Beating Parma to qualify for the Champions League group stage the following season might have been it but we were drawn in a fearsome group that had Bayern Munich, who had just lost the final to Manchester United, and Valencia, who would reach the next two Champions League finals. There was also Advocaat's former team, PSV Eindhoven, whom we beat home and away.

I didn't start any of the six games or the UEFA Cup tie against Borussia Dortmund that followed. My biggest contribution was 53 minutes against Valencia at Ibrox. We were unlucky in both the games against Bayern Munich. We should have beaten them at Ibrox but Michael Tarnat equalised with a late free kick. In the return at the Olympic Stadium, Michael Mols collided with Oliver

Kahn and tore his cruciate ligaments.

Mols was another of Advocaat's Dutch signings, this time from Utrecht, but he was one of the best. Earlier in the season, he had scored all four against Motherwell and he had scored two when Eindhoven were beaten 4–1 at Ibrox.

He was 28 then and was a footballer at his peak. Celtic lost Henrik Larsson to a horrible double fracture at Lyons at around the same time but while Larsson recovered, Mols was never the same player.

If the draw for the Champions League was hard, so was the one for the UEFA Cup: Rangers got Borussia Dortmund. We won the first leg 2–0, lost the second by the same score and went out on penalties.

I was brought on for extra time in the Westfalenstadion, although I wasn't among the five chosen to take a penalty. Jens Lehmann, who had helped Dortmund score their stoppage-time equaliser when he came up for a corner, saved three of our penalties.

I didn't take many in my career. I remember one for Everton in an FA Cup tie against Swindon in 1997 when one of their defenders, Ian Culverhouse, was sent off for handling my shot in the area after 52 seconds.

People talk about nerves when you take a penalty but whenever I did step up to take one I told myself that if I hit it hard and aimed for a corner, the goalkeeper would have no chance.

The best penalty-taker I ever came across was Igor Dobrovolski, who was part of the Soviet Union side that won the football tournament in our last Olympics, in Seoul in 1988. He scored six times in all, including one against Brazil in the final, and in that tournament only Romario scored more.

Dobrovolski's career was largely before the age of video analysis when a goalkeeper would study an opponent's penalty-taker. Dobrovolski always struck his penalties in the same place and almost invariably the keeper would go the wrong way.

He left the Soviet Union at the same time as Mikhailichenko and Baltacha but although he played for some big clubs like Marseilles and Atletico Madrid he never settled at any of them and what should have been a great career petered out in Dusseldorf.

I played for three seasons in the Champions League and did not get out of the group in any of them. The last season was probably the most disappointing. This time we were drawn in a straightforward group: Monaco, Galatasaray and Sturm Graz. We thrashed Graz 5–0 at Ibrox and beat Monaco 1–0 away. Six points from two games should have propelled us into the knockout stages.

By the time we went to Istanbul in late September, I had played all my football off the bench. Rangers had not been playing well in the Scottish Premier League. Martin O'Neill's first derby had seen Celtic win 6–2 and we were third in the table. But if we beat Galatasaray home or away we would probably be favourites to reach the knockout rounds.

The Ali Sami Yen was exactly as I remembered it from my time with Manchester United. The chanting started an hour before the game, the sheer aggression that eclipsed even Celtic Park, but in one respect it was different: it was pouring down. It was raining in hell.

Advocaat put me on after an hour when Galatasaray were two up. Soon it was three. I scored with a header and Giovanni van Bronckhorst delivered one of his trademark free kicks but it was too late.

I thought Advocaat was far too defensive when Galatasaray came to Glasgow. I don't think he trusted his defenders any more. Amoruso had lost form and was suspended and Bert Konterman, who had been brought in from Feyenoord in the summer, was having a rough time. Advocaat planned for a 1–0 win and got a 0–0 draw.

The last wave of his Dutch signings were expensive and not up to scratch. Konterman was not nearly as good as Colin Hendry, the man he replaced in the Rangers defence. We had heard that Hendry had been signed by David Murray because he wanted Scottish footballers in the Rangers squad but Advocaat barely played him. That, to me, shows what a good chairman Murray, was because he was more in touch with the concerns of his dressing room than his manager.

Towards the end, when Rangers' debt was becoming a real concern, he tried to rein Advocaat back because he was buying players the club did not need, want or could afford. Ronald de Boer was one of them.

De Boer had arrived at Ibrox from Barcelona with a huge reputation. However, he was thirty when he signed and had constant problems with his knees. After every game he was unable to train for two days and you often saw De Boer in the dressing room with ice-packs on his knees.

Advocaat's obsession with Dutch footballers meant that sometimes it felt we started with nine men because one, Konterman, was not good enough and the other, De Boer, was not fit enough for regular first-team football.

Often we could get away with it in the Scottish Premier League but in one month, October 2000, we lost 3–0 at home to Kilmarnock, 2–1 at St Johnstone and 1–0 at Hibernian. In the Champions

162

League we became more and more exposed.

The last two European games were disastrous. We went to Austria and lost 2–0 to Sturm Graz. Sergei Yuran, who had been with me at Dynamo Kiev, scored the opening goal. He was from Luhansk in eastern Ukraine, a tearaway who always seemed to be disciplined by Valery Lobanovsky. Yuran had a problem with alcohol throughout his career, particularly when he went to Millwall.

He was in the same under-21 team as me that won the European Championship for the Soviet Union in 1990 and, like me, he was a Ukrainian who chose Russia. But he was also one of those who signed the letter saying they would not go to the 1994 World Cup and then changed their mind. We had a very similar upbringing but it was then that our paths diverged.

It meant we had to beat Monaco at Ibrox to go through. We were leading with twelve minutes to go when Amoruso made his mistake to allow Marco Simone to score. He lost the captaincy and we were making a familiar journey to play a German side in the UEFA Cup. I didn't go to Kaiserslautern because by then I had had my training-ground fight with Fernando Ricksen and been banished by Advocaat. Kaiserslautern beat Rangers easily. That, too, was familiar.

There were times when I really enjoyed myself at Rangers; when I could play and smile. In February 1999 we beat Dunfermline 3–0 at Ibrox and Rod Wallace sent in a high deep cross that I struck on the volley into the top corner of the net. At the time it was compared to something Marco van Basten might have done ten years before.

A year later, Rangers were playing Ayr in the Scottish Cup semi-final at Hampden Park. It was a no-contest. Rangers won 7–0 and Billy Dodds, who came on as a half-time substitute, scored a hat-trick. When the ball came to me in the middle of Ayr's half, I jumped on it with both feet, balanced myself on top of it and put my hand to my eyes as if I were looking for someone to pass to.

The commentator at the semi-final had warned viewers not to try this at home but one youngster had attempted to do it, fallen off and broken his arm.

When we made the final of the Scottish FA Cup in 2000, Advocaat's superiority complex was at its zenith. We had won the league easily and were playing Aberdeen, who had finished bottom of the Premier League, a full 57 points behind us.

As the final approached, a movement grew up among the Rangers fans for everyone to wear orange at Hampden Park as a tribute to Advocaat's role in transforming the club. It was enthusiastically taken up by the club's marketing department, who helped produce thousands of orange shirts for the final, and Advocaat actually wanted the team to wear them in the final.

As an outsider, I only associated orange with the Dutch football team but in Glasgow politics orange is the colour of the Protestant majority and many wondered if there were deeper, darker meanings behind it. All I know is that none of us wanted to go out at Hampden wearing orange shirts. We played in the traditional blue of Glasgow Rangers and won 4–0.

It was the same scoreline as Manchester United's victory over Chelsea in the FA Cup final six years before and it was even more one-sided. The game was probably beyond Aberdeen anyway but in the first couple of minutes I sent over a low cross for Rod Wallace; he collided with the Aberdeen keeper, Jim Leighton, who was taken off with a broken jaw.

Aberdeen did not have a reserve keeper on the bench so one of their strikers, Robbie Winters, had to go in goal. His job was like trying to stop a steamroller. We went up the steps at Hampden to collect Glasgow Rangers' one hundredth trophy. It was the last the club would win under Dick Advocaat.

12
THE SECRET LIFE OF ARABIA

IT WOULD BE A DOUBLE-SIDED REUNION. I WOULD BE returning to Manchester and I would be working again with Joe Royle. I was at Rangers on the fringes of the team when Joe phoned me and asked me if I wanted to join Manchester City on loan.

They had been promoted the previous season but now it was January and they were deep in the relegation zone. Joe said I was not playing much in Scotland so what did I have to lose?

Joe Royle was a man I knew and liked. One supporter had posted him a gadget with a red switch in the middle on which was written the words: 'Panic Button'. But there were fourteen games left and there was only a three-point gap between Manchester City and safety. Perhaps I could make a difference?

My first game was at home to Liverpool. I was brought on in the second half, Danny Tiatto scored an equaliser and I really enjoyed playing in a fixture that had brought me so much success.

We played Liverpool again in the FA Cup in February, this time at Anfield. I scored from the edge of the area but City were already two goals down and we ended up losing 4–2. But we won at Newcastle, thanks to a goal from Shaun Goater. Newcastle had prepared for the match by flying to Spain for some warm-weather training at La Manga. We were one point off safety.

Manchester City were soon planning their own trip to Spain. We were no longer in the FA Cup and there was a two-week break between games, but I am certain that if we had stayed at home we would have had a better chance of survival.

We flew to Marbella. I was sharing a room with a French defender, Laurent Charvet, and we went over to Steve Howey's room to ask if he wanted to come with us to get something to eat. Having seen the Rangers players pack out the Marbella branch of McDonald's, I wanted to take some City players to a proper restaurant.

Howey was lying on his bed watching television and all around him he had bottles of beer. 'Do you want to come for some food?' I asked him. Steve pointed to one bottle: 'That's my breakfast.' Then he pointed to another. 'That's my lunch, and that bottle over there; that's my dinner.'

Laurent and I went to find a restaurant and at around eight o'clock we came back and looked in on Steve. He was still lying on his bed. He hadn't moved; he had just called room service and all around him was a mass of empty beer bottles.

Steve Howey was a good player for Manchester City and a good guy but I couldn't believe he didn't want to leave the hotel and at least see something of Marbella. 'No,' he replied, gesturing around the room. 'I've got everything I need here.'

Manchester City had played quite well before we went to Marbella but when we got back our focus had gone. We lost three games in succession that culminated in a home game with Arsenal, where we were four goals down before half-time.

Had the squad remained in England and trained hard at Platt Lane, we would have been much better prepared for the final, crucial games of the season. In Spain we barely trained at all.

It was as tough for Royle at Manchester City as it had been in his final season at Everton. His wife and father were both seriously ill and the club could not be pulled clear of the relegation zone.

On 21 April 2001, a decade after I flew from Donetsk to Manchester to sign for Alex Ferguson, I played my last game at Old Trafford.

It was a strange derby. Manchester United had just won the championship with five games to spare while City were third-bottom, five points from safety, having played one match more than the two teams above us. They were top of the heap, we were going down.

We actually drew 1–1 but the game is now only remembered for one incident: Roy Keane's wild, premeditated tackle on Alf-Inge Haaland. We didn't know it then but this was Keane's punishment on Haaland for suggesting he was play-acting when he had torn his cruciate ligaments against Leeds four years before. Keane had a long memory – at the time we just thought he had gone crazy. He didn't even wait for the red card.

That was my final game for Manchester City. They were relegated, Royle was sacked and I returned to Glasgow Rangers.

I was 32 now but Celtic, under Martin O'Neill, had won the Scottish Premier League by fifteen points and, if Rangers were serious about winning it back in 2001/02, I felt I had a lot to offer. Rangers felt differently. I spent a lot of time on the bench and I didn't start a game until the 2–2 draw at Hearts on 8 September, six games into the season. My next start was also against Hearts and that was in April. Mostly, I was on the bench or out of the squad.

Rangers lost the league by an even greater margin than they had in 2001 – this time it was eighteen points. In December, Dick Advocaat had resigned and was replaced by Alex McLeish. Briefly, I thought my career might be about to flicker back into life.

I found McLeish two-faced. When he spoke to me he was encouraging, saying he had confidence in me and that I could make a real contribution to the second half of the season, but I found out afterwards that he went to the chairman, David Murray, and said he wanted rid of me.

My final match for Rangers was spectacular, a 1–1 draw at Celtic Park that saw three players sent off in the final minute in a massed fight. It seemed an appropriate way to say goodbye, with the passion that Valery Lobanovsky had talked about in that video in Kiev all those years ago spilling over into a punch-up.

I was now a free agent. I had to find a club and my next move was from Glasgow to Brighton, who had just been promoted to the First Division in England. Steve Coppell asked if I wanted to train with the team but just as he was about to offer me a contract, I was told that Southampton wanted to take me on.

However, I was told while the chairman, Rupert Lowe, was interested, his manager, Gordon Strachan, wasn't that keen on the idea; but I phoned Strachan and asked if I could come down and train. Eventually, Southampton signed me on a short-term contract.

Training was virtually all I did. I had a house in Sussex and I drove down to the training ground. It was one hour twenty minutes there, one hour twenty minutes back. In terms of Russian distances it was not too bad. There were a couple of games but my information that Strachan had not been the one behind the signing was accurate.

I was still at Southampton, nowhere near the first team, wondering what to do with what was left of my career when, in January 2003, I got a call from an agent called Sandor Varga. He was from Hungary, his wife was Russian and he had worked with Oleg Luzhny and Sergei Rebrov. He had been living in Saudi Arabia for many years and he asked if I would be interested in playing for Al-Hilal.

The club's name translates as 'The Crescent Moon' and it is the biggest and best-supported team in the country. It was based in Riyadh and had the backing of the Saudi royal family.

I played about a dozen games for Al-Hilal and we won the Crown Prince Cup, the Saudi equivalent of the FA Cup. I lived in a compound for foreigners in Riyadh. The British, the French and the Americans all had their own compound and there were schools, shops and restaurants, while the apartments had a swimming pool. It was cut off from the rest of the capital; a little world for those who were not from Saudi Arabia.

The heat dominated everything. Saudi Arabia was a totally different world; a country where things happened at night. The working day began at five in the evening and ended around ten or eleven. You would go to bed at dawn and get up at about three. Training began at eight after prayers.

During the day you would either stay indoors or move from an air-conditioned apartment to an air-conditioned car that would drive you to another air-conditioned building. After a couple of months, you began to think that 36 degrees was pretty cool.

The only problem was that you couldn't drink, which wasn't a problem for me but it might have been for some of those I shared a dressing room with in England. I wasn't shocked by how much English footballers drank when I was in the Premier League – the Soviet Union was notorious for how much alcohol people put away.

What surprised me was that they didn't eat while they drank. In the beer bars of the Soviet Union there would always be a plate of salt fish to hand, and as people got wealthier there might be prawns or crayfish. In England there was only one thing on the menu – straight beer.

Few, however, touched cigarettes, while in Italy lighting up was more tolerated than if you opened a can of beer or went off for fast food. Fiorentina always encouraged you to have a glass of wine with your meal. When I broke into the Soviet Union's national team in 1991, I discovered I was the only non-smoker.

Walking into the dressing room was like entering a pub. When we were in hotels waiting to go to the game, I used to have to ask them to go out on to the balcony if they wanted a cigarette.

You could get alcohol in Saudi Arabia, if you knew the right kind of local; if you wanted a beer, one could be arranged. The biggest drinkers of all were some members of the Saudi family. Because it was forbidden for the police to enter the home of a member of the royal family, some had huge stocks of alcohol in their palaces. They would take trips to Bahrain or London to party. In all my years in football I had never seen anyone drink so much as some of those Saudi princes.

Al-Hilal employed a couple of foreigners, including the Cameroon forward, Patrick Suffo, who had played for Sheffield United, and the managers were foreign. I was only at Al-Hilal for a short while but I still had two managers. The first was Ilie Balaci, a great Romanian footballer, who had spent years managing in the Arab world.

He was replaced by Aad de Mos, who had won the Dutch Eredivisie with Ajax and won the Cup Winners' Cup in 1988 with Mechelen by beating Ajax in the final. After all my problems with Dick Advocaat, I thought it funny that I had come all this way to be managed by another Dutchman, but I found De Mos to be one of the good guys.

The coaching was done in English. Al-Hilal's greatest player was their centre-forward, Sami Al-Jaber, who scored more than 100 goals for the club. He was still leading their attack and had spent several months on loan at Wolves, so he was able to translate for me if anything was said in Arabic.

When you went outside the compound, you were struck by just how different it was. For a capital city, Riyadh was very quiet, except for the call to prayer that rang out five times a day. Everyone wore Islamic dress, which made you stand out even more as a foreigner.

When my wife, Inna, came over to visit she would wear a headscarf. What Saudi women wore depended on what their husbands wanted. Their dress reflected the requests of their men. Sometimes it would be a hijab, sometimes a full burka. In Saudi Arabia, the schools would close when the temperatures reached forty degrees. For reasons I was never able to work out, the official temperatures in Riyadh never went above 39.8.

For someone living in one of the wealthiest countries in the world, I came across a lot of very poor people. Some houses did not even have electricity. If you went inside, you would see homes lit by oil lamps.

The president of Al-Hilal was a member of the Saudi royal family, Prince Abdullah. He had been educated in the United States, was a big fan of American football and he spoke perfect English.

The Saudi royal family would never invite you into their homes – only relatives were allowed in – but I would be invited to a camp in the desert or a guest house, where you would be given everything you could possibly need.

I would go out there and play chess or darts or cards with Prince Abdullah until four in the morning. I'd long been interested in chess. I have a plan to open the kind of sports boarding school that I went to in Kharkov and, if that ever comes to fruition, I would have chess on the curriculum. Chess teaches you a lot about tactics and lateral thinking.

Chess was very popular in the Soviet Union, not least because Lenin had been a fan of the game. The day before a match, the whole team would go to the training ground, where they would rest, eat and sleep before the match, and each training ground would have its own chess tables.

There would also be billiard tables and places where you'd play cards or backgammon, but they were very keen on the footballers to play chess because it encouraged them to think. There were no PlayStations, no mobile phones and no internet to help pass the time.

When I was at Manchester United a pack of cards was the key to killing time. Steve Bruce, Bryan Robson and I often played cards on the bus and sometimes Alex Ferguson would come up to the back for a few hands of brag.

In Russia we would play Durak, where the aim is to get rid of all your cards. You didn't bet on it but the last player with cards in his hand would be the *durak* or 'fool'.

The highlight of my time in Saudi Arabia was the final of the Crown Prince Cup, a Riyadh derby between Al-Hilal and Al-Ahli, which we won 1–0 in front of about 40,000. Normally, the crowds would be about 10,000, with no women allowed into the stadium. They weren't even allowed to drive a car. If you went into a department store, there would be a single floor for women only; the rest of the store would be for men.

There were rules that were equally bizarre. They would allow you to take photographs with a normal camera but not with a mobile phone equipped with a camera. If you bought a mobile phone in Saudi Arabia, it would already have had its camera removed.

The attitude to life was different. Death was regarded as routine, something almost unworthy of comment. You would hear stories, told matter-of-factly, about people who had been on the Hajj to Mecca and who had stumbled, fallen and been crushed to death as a sea of people walked around the big, black cube of the Kaaba.

It might seem callous to non-Islamic eyes, but to die on the Hajj confers in Saudi Arabia a kind of privilege. If you die within the walls of Mecca, you go straight to heaven.

I don't know where those who were executed in Deera Square went. I was once asked if I wanted to go to a public execution of eighteen Filipinos who had been convicted of drug trafficking. Naturally, I said no.

Deera Square – or 'Chop-Chop Square' as the locals called it – was where Riyadh staged its beheadings. They were held on a Friday after morning prayers. It is all designed to make the penalties of the Saudi justice system very clear.

If it were an 'execution Friday', a substantial crowd would be guaranteed. It would be less than would come to watch the football in the King Fahd Stadium but the square would still be pretty packed. It was regarded as both a spectacle and as an education.

It was a strange land but one I could negotiate my way through and one in which I might have stayed longer but for the intervention of Al-Qaeda.

On the night 12 May 2003 there were co-ordinated attacks against Western compounds across Riyadh. They hit the Dorrat Al-Jawadel, which was owned by one of Saudi Arabia's wealthiest businessmen, the hotelier, Mohamed Al-Jaber.

Then a truck and a BMW pulled up outside the Oasis Village at Al-Hawra. The explosives inside the truck were set off and the buildings were sprayed with bullets from AK47s fired by the men in the car, who were dressed as security guards.

Then they attacked the Vinnell complex, which housed Americans who trained the Saudi Royal Guard. By the end of the night there were 39 dead and 160 injured.

I was playing chess with Prince Abdullah in his camp when the attacks began and I knew nothing of the bloodshed until the next morning when Inna called from Moscow. When I asked why there was this panic in her voice, she said, 'Haven't you been watching the news?' One of the compounds Al-Qaeda had attacked was near to where I was living. Any foreigner who lived in Saudi Arabia was now a legitimate target. I packed my bags and flew back to Moscow the next morning.

It was a long time since I had flown to Russia to play international football. My last competitive game had been against Ukraine in 1998, a qualifier for the European Championships in Holland and Belgium. We lost 3–2 to a Ukraine side that was spearheaded by Andriy Shevchenko and Sergei Rebrov, the players who would take Dynamo Kiev to the semi-finals of the Champions League.

It was played in Kiev and, looking back, there is a certain symbolism to the fact that my last game should have been playing against the country where I was born, playing in the city where I learned my football. At the time, I didn't know it was the end. Footballers rarely do.

19
HERDING THE RAMS

IN RUSSIAN, JAROSLAV HREBIK WOULD BE KNOWN AS a 'ram'. He was stubborn, he was stupid and he was aggressive. He was comfortably the worst manager I have ever worked with.

Twelve years after leaving for Manchester, I returned to live in Moscow permanently. I had signed a two-year contract to be Dynamo Moscow's captain and I would help Hrebik out with some coaching.

Hrebik managed Dynamo between stints at Sparta Prague and he was big on fitness. He would have two training sessions a day, each lasting for three hours. We had to do one exercise constantly for forty minutes. His other big idea was that all the players should keep close to each other as if they were on a basketball pitch.

His big idea didn't work very well since Dynamo Moscow fin-

179

ished one point above a relegation place in 2004, although Hrebik was gone long before the season finished. He was told his job was to take Dynamo into the top three of the Russian Premier League. As soon as I saw his primitive training methods, I told Hrebik they would be lucky to stay out of the bottom three. They finished third-bottom. Fortunately for Dynamo, only the bottom two went down.

Hrebik lasted four months, although had he stayed, Dynamo would have been relegated for the first time in their history. They brought in Oleg Romantsev to dig themselves out of trouble.

I had left Dynamo long before Hrebik. Once more it involved a trip to Marbella. The team had gone to Spain to prepare for the 2004 season, which began in March. We stayed in the hills above the town. One night we wanted to take a taxi into Marbella. There were a couple of cabs outside the hotel but the first driver we asked said no. It was too far and too late. I was given the task of trying to negotiate a fare.

I spoke Italian, the driver replied in Spanish. It developed into an argument and while we were arguing the second taxi driver struck me with a baseball bat. The blow cracked a rib. Some of the Dynamo players threatened to call the police and the taxis drove off into the night.

One of the reasons why we were so keen to go out was because we didn't think there would be a training session the next day. However, the next morning, Hrebik said he wanted us out on the pitch.

I had a broken rib that would not stand up to one of Hrebik's three-hour marathons but I did not dare tell the manager how I had come to be injured. 'I have a sore back, I can't train,' I told him. He accused me of trying to get out of the session because I didn't fancy it.

Things came to a head on our last night before flying back to Moscow. Because the training camp was over, we were sitting on the terrace outside a bar. We'd had a bit to drink, nothing spectacular, but we were spotted by one of Hrebik's assistants.

He informed the manager and Hrebik told Dynamo's president that there had been a breach of club discipline. I was 35, which was old for a footballer in Russia. Many coaches there still had the same Soviet mentality that a player should have retired by the time he was 31.

Generally, Russian managers were suspicious of players with experience. Hrebik was Czech but his attitude was Russian. Dynamo Moscow had a young squad and I was seen as a threat and a source of alternative advice.

When we got back to Russia, I was told to see the president, Yuri Zavarzin, and was accused of leading the whole Dynamo squad astray by taking them out drinking and of refusing to train.

Zavarzin decided my contract would be cancelled and I would be transferred to FC Saturn, which was also in the Russian Premier League but located in Ramenskoye, in the suburbs, south-east of Moscow.

Ramenskoye was a short 45-minute drive away and Saturn was managed by a man I knew, Boris Ignatiev. He had been Romantsev's assistant with Russia during Euro 96 and took over after the tournament. He was the national manager when we just failed to qualify for the 1998 World Cup and the man who had tried to persuade me to play with a broken kneecap.

His team at Saturn included a lot of foreigners, mainly South Americans. We were not playing well, were sliding towards relegation and one of our crucial fixtures was at Rotor Volgograd, who would finish bottom of the Russian Premier League.

Volgograd is much better known by its former name. Stalingrad. Once we were in the away dressing room, Ignatiev decided to make a big speech. 'You know where we are, boys. We're in Stalingrad. The tide of history turned here when the Russians refused to yield an inch of soil to the Germans. What the citizens of Stalingrad did in 1942, you must do now.'

His words were translated for the South Americans. They all turned to each other and began whispering. 'What is this Stalingrad? What happened here?' They had no idea what he was talking about. We lost the game 1–0 and Ignatiev lost his job soon afterwards.

The standards may have dropped but in one respect Russian football was pretty much like Soviet football. The Premier League always seemed to have the same managers; they simply managed different clubs.

It was very hard for a young coach to get a break with a big team. Ignatiev was replaced by Alexander Tarkhanov, who had previously managed CSKA and Torpedo Moscow. His big idea was to use deflated footballs in training. It was popular in Brazil, particularly on the beaches, Tarkhanov explained. Curiously, we didn't play like Brazilians. The Moscow region is short on beaches.

It says everything about the Russian game that Hrebik with his three-hour training sessions and Tarkhanov with his deflated footballs were Premier League managers.

It was not just the football that was different in Russia. For the first time since leaving for Manchester thirteen years before, I was back home. It was a very different city and a very different country that I returned to. Football in Russia had changed but life itself had changed. There were new shops and restaurants everywhere, you could go out and expect a good meal rather than be surprised by one.

We had owned an apartment in Moscow for some years. Inna and the family had lived there while I was in Saudi Arabia and I had used it when I was playing for the Russian national team.

When I started playing for Dynamo Kiev in 1988, football in the Soviet Union could be counted as one of the top five leagues in Europe. Maybe, we liked to think, it could be counted among the top three.

The standard had dropped alarmingly by the time I signed my contract to play for Dynamo Moscow and it has fallen further still. There is only one Russian footballer now playing in the major leagues in the West.

Denis Cheryshev grew up in Spain, where his father, Dmitri, played for Sporting Gijon. Denis had his football education at the Real Madrid academy and has played his whole career in La Liga. The only time he goes to Russia is when he plays for the national team and that tells its own story.

There is no interest in Russian footballers in western Europe. There is no market for them. There are Russian clubs that have money – Zenit St Petersburg, Spartak and CSKA Moscow – but Russian football is not profitable, which is why the country's oligarchs, the Abramoviches and the Usmanovs, tend to look abroad.

Sergey Galitsky, who owns Magnit, took over FC Krasnodar but that was because he grew up in the city. They have spent £170m on a new stadium, money I don't think Galitsky will be getting back.

My final games as a player were in Samara, playing for Krylia Sovetov. The name means 'Wings of the Soviets'. I knew the manager there, a man called Gadzhi Gadzhiyev, who had been an assistant in the Russian national team.

He was from Dagestan, a region by the Caspian Sea in the far south of Russia that was disfigured by communal violence. He was to manage Dagestan's principal club, Anzhi Makhachkala, on five separate occasions.

Samara was far enough east to have been designated the capital of the Soviet Union should the Germans have occupied Moscow in 1941. It's a two-hour flight from the capital, which to a Russian is a short trip.

During my time playing in Russia, Luch Energia Vladivostok were promoted to the Russian Premier League. Their stadium is on the shores of the Sea of Japan. Getting there from Moscow involves a flight of eight or nine hours across seven time zones.

When Zenit St Petersburg were due to play away at Vladivostok, a group of Zenit fans decided to drive the 6,500 miles to Luch Energia's stadium in a twenty-year-old Honda. Their team won 2–0, but the car broke down in Vladivostok and they had to take the Trans-Siberian Railway to get home. When they arrived Zenit presented them with a new car. The old one is on display in the club museum.

In winter Samara could be freezing. During one match in November the temperature fell to minus-fifteen. Believe me, you have to play a game of football at fifteen-below to know what it feels like. We kept going over to the referee, begging him to reduce the game to forty minutes a half just to allow us back into the dressing rooms.

The president of Krylia Sovetov was a man called Baranov. In Russian, Baranov means 'like a ram', and he had all the ram-like qualities – stubbornness, aggression and stupidity – that Jaroslav Hrebik had brought to Dynamo Moscow.

When I was looking to end my playing career, I suggested I might be able to arrange a friendly with Manchester United. Baranov looked at me and said, 'What are Manchester United?'

We finished ninth in the Russian Premier League. I had played well and enjoyed the football and started twenty-two out of thirty league matches, but Krylia had brought in a new manager, Sergei Oborin, who told me he wanted to promote younger players.

That is a laudable sentiment but every team requires a mix of ages for it to function properly. People still talk about how Alex Ferguson's kids won the Double for Manchester United in 1996. However, although Scholes, Beckham, Butt and Neville played very well, Ferguson also needed older talents, men like Bruce, Cantona and Schmeichel.

Without their more experienced players, Krylia began the season badly and Oborin was fired after a few months. His next job was in Siberia.

I hadn't any clear idea of what I would do once the football finished but actually stopping was painful. You missed the rush of match days and it also coincided with my divorce from Inna. The days were slow.

I did go to the 2008 Champions League final between Manchester United and Chelsea that was being staged at the Luzhniki in Moscow. That team was, I think, the only one Sir Alex Ferguson built that really compares to the 1994 side. Ryan Giggs, astonishingly, played for both.

We were more disciplined than the side of Rooney, Ronaldo and Carlos Tevez. We kept our shape better. They were more fluid but our midfield was better, with men like Roy Keane and Paul Ince, and we had good, old-school defenders, men like Steve Bruce and

Denis Irwin. It would have been a good contest between the two sides but I think our team was better.

Before the final, I went to the Manchester United team hotel to see the players and wish them good luck. My son, Andrei, was a teenager by then and I brought him along. I was talking to Gary Neville when he stopped the conversation dead and pointed to Andrei, who was standing behind me, wearing a Manchester United shirt.

'What are you doing here, boy, can't you see we're having a conversation?' he said to Andrei. 'I don't want any fans hanging about the place. Please, just fuck off.'

'But, Gary,' I said. 'This is my son.'

I did not want to go looking for another club at 38 but I still wanted to be part of football, and I was offered the post of general manager of a club called Nosta Novotroitsk. It was a long way from Moscow, on the edge of Russia itself, where the Ural mountains border Kazakhstan.

After Adolf Hitler unleashed Operation Barbarossa on the Soviet Union in 1941, Stalin ordered factories in western Russia to be dismantled and shipped east. The steel plants were sent to Novotroitsk, which is now the headquarters of Ural Stal.

There, the blast furnaces burn 24 hours a day, every day. The temperatures are so intense that, if you turned them off, it would take months to get them back to the required levels.

There were so many chemicals and so much waste at the plant that you could find every element in the periodic table there. In winter, the snow was red because so much stuff had been pumped into the air since the factories opened more than half a century ago.

Nearby were factories producing cement and bricks. Novotroitsk was totally functional, totally committed to heavy industry. It was a city of 112,000 people, which didn't possess a cinema, though I do recall that the trams were free.

It was about the size of Blackburn and, for a Russian city, Novotroitsk was tiny. If you want a sense of how big a city is in Russian terms, you need to divide the total by ten. Novotroitsk was a village, a dirty, fume-filled village that had not changed since Soviet times. People died at fifty.

You would hear stories of workers going home exhausted from the steelworks, arguing with their wives or getting drunk on vodka. The next morning they would get up, go to work and then throw themselves into the furnace. Long before they got anywhere near the flames, the 400-degree temperatures would evaporate their bodies, turning them instantly to ash, to nothing.

The club was owned by Alisher Usmanov, who now owns a big chunk of Arsenal, but the Metallurg Stadium with its capacity of 6,000 was nothing like the Emirates. As the general manager, I was in charge, not just on the pitch, but of arranging transfers and running the club.

It was while I was working for him at Novotroitsk that Usmanov began to be interested in Arsenal, and Sandor Varga and I helped him to buy his 27 per cent share of the club.

Usmanov grew up in Tashkent in Uzbekistan; he went to prison when it was part of the Soviet Union and he is a Muslim whose wife is Jewish. He made his money making plastic bags, which were scarce in the Soviet Union, before becoming involved in steel making and mining after the Soviet Union broke up. He is not a one-dimensional oligarch. His love of football is genuine. Why else would you become involved with Nosta Novotroitsk?

Because of the almost complete lack of anything to do and the problems with pollution and radiation, attracting footballers to Novotroitsk was, to put it mildly, somewhat difficult. The main attraction for some of them seemed to be my name and the fact that we had to offer them more money than they could get elsewhere. The referees, too, were on the lookout for money. One asked me how much I was prepared to pay to settle the result. I sent him away.

When trying to bring players to Novotroitsk, I kept recalling Joe Royle's comment when I told him I was thinking of signing for Middlesbrough. 'What do you want to go there for? It's like Chernobyl.'

However, despite that, we finished fifth in what would be the Russian equivalent of the Championship. Nosta played some good football, although I used to fly back to Moscow during gaps in the fixture list. It was not a place that encouraged you to linger.

The club was in a kind of permanent chaos and in the end Novotroitsk were relegated and I was back in Moscow, at Torpedo Zil. This time I would be running just the first team rather than the whole club.

The story of Torpedo Zil tells you a lot about Russia after the fall of the Soviet Union. Zil made cars that were the Rolls-Royces of the Soviet empire. They were the cars in which the leaders of the country were driven around in, often in what were called Zil Lanes – a part of a dual carriageway that was reserved exclusively for Soviet dignitaries.

The cars were made in Moscow and they sponsored Torpedo. They were one of the great names of Soviet football that boasted one of its greatest talents, Eduard Streltsov.

He was a fabulous striker who just before the 1958 World Cup was convicted of rape and sent to the gulag. There are those who believe that the real reason was that he had finished a relationship with the daughter of Ekaterina Furtseva, a powerful member of the politburo.

He returned after five years of hard labour and led Torpedo to the 1965 Soviet championship. There were few high points after that. Zil split from the football club. Torpedo moved from its little stadium to the vastness of the Luzhniki, where it played in front of 75,000 empty seats. They were relegated two divisions.

Zil launched their own club, which they called Torpedo Zil, and were given financial backing by one of Boris Yeltsin's advisors, Alexander Mamut, who now owns the Waterstone's bookshops. They kept Torpedo Moscow's old stadium and renamed it after Streltsov.

Torpedo Zil won promotion to the Russian Premier League but the money began to run out and they were sold, taken over by the city council and renamed FK Moscow. Then in 2003 another club was launched called Torpedo Zil, and this was the one that I joined seven years later. Complicated? Sure, everything in Russian football was becoming complicated.

Torpedo Zil were in the third tier of Russian football, where they had finished fourteenth. It would have been nice to have started a coaching career at one of the big clubs but I had to begin somewhere and I didn't feel I could pick and choose. I needed experience.

I had been managed by men like Valery Lobanovsky, Alex Ferguson and Claudio Ranieri – I took little things from them but my coaching drew most of all on my own experiences. I had been a winger. I liked wingers and I wanted my teams to have them.

The trouble was I was working with people who had very little idea of what a winger was. The chairman of Torpedo Zil was a man called Vitaly Chernyshyov, who knew absolutely nothing about football. His sporting director, a man called Donyets, thought he knew about football because he had read some books about the game.

Their star player was Denis Yevsikov, who had won the Russian Premier League with CSKA Moscow and was easily the highest-paid member of the squad. The trouble was, he didn't fit into the team I was trying to create.

One day I was approached by Chernyshyov, who said, 'I need you to play Yevsikov in the next match.'

'I can't. He is not remotely what we need.'

'If you don't, I will suspend you.'

'Here is the whistle. If you know that much about football, why don't you take the next training session?'

Chernyshyov backed down but it was hard to keep him at bay for long. We were drawing the next match 1–1 when he wandered down from his hospitality box in the stadium and walked across to the bench. He called out to me and my assistant: 'If you don't win this game, I am going to fire you.'

'Why don't you go back to your box, keep on drinking your whisky and we'll manage the players,' I yelled back at him. We won the match 2–1.

The club arranged a photo-call to smooth out the differences between us. The photograph they published had each of us looking away from the other.

Because of the size of Russia, the Second Division – the equivalent of League One in England – was divided into five regions. We came second in our regional group. At the same time my old club,

Saturn Moscow, had been engulfed by a financial crisis. They could no longer pay their players and in 2010 the club folded.

Their place in the Russian Premier League was taken by Krasnodar, which left a vacancy in the National Football League – the equivalent of the Championship.

We applied for it, as did another club, Fakel Voronezh. The year before, Fakel had been expelled from the Second Division for attempting to bribe a referee. They got round this by simply forming a new club, which looked very much like the old club. It had the same manager and the same name. Torpedo Zil finished second while Voronezh finished fourth. We didn't pay any money to the authorities while Voronezh offered some 'financial guarantees'. They were promoted.

Torpedo Zil's owner, Alexander Mamut, was so disgusted that he announced he no longer wanted to be involved in football. I am sure he was offered the same opportunity to make some 'financial guarantees' but he couldn't believe sport had come to this, so he refused.

Mamut simply pulled the plug on the club, which overnight ceased to exist. There was no point trying to get him to reverse the decision. Alexander Mamut was a man who did not change his mind.

I cannot pretend that my involvement with Torpedo Zil was a happy time, at least off the pitch. The chairman and his sporting director formed one group while my backroom staff and I formed another. We hardly ever mingled but then one day we were at Riga airport in Latvia waiting for a flight when I decided to go and have a chat with Donyets. During the conversation I told him I was writing a book called *Returning to Russia* about my experiences since coming home. Donyets turned to me and said, 'Don't write anything bad about me.'

I had to disappoint him.

The moment Torpedo Zil folded, I and everyone else connected with the organisation had to find a new club, which is how I came to end up giving a half-time team talk while my sporting director burst in brandishing a baseball bat.

The man's name was Shamil Gazizov and the club was FC Ufa. He was shouting at the players that, unless their performances started improving, he would start using the baseball bat on them. I told him to get out.

I had always been taught that when you manage a team you should treat its players like members of your own family. You can express your disappointment with them; you can praise them, encourage them and warn them. But you can't beat them up.

Gazizov had competed in the Olympic pentathlon for the Soviet Union so he should have had some idea of how sportsmen operate, but that was the calibre of some of the people working in Russian football.

Ufa was a big, largely ignored city. The countryside that surrounds it with its lakes and mountains is stunning but Ufa itself is modern and with not much architecture to talk about.

It is the capital of Bashkortostan, a mainly Islamic republic in the foothills of the Urals. The club is now part of the Russian Premier League but when I went there Ufa were a freshly formed club in the third tier of Russian football in the regional Ural-Povolzhye Zone.

We finished second in my first and only season in Bashkortostan. Apart from a sporting director who liked to make his point with a baseball bat, Ufa's biggest problem was that the city's great sporting passion was ice hockey.

The ice hockey team was called Salavat Yulaev, named after one of the heroes of the great Cossack uprising in the eighteenth century. When I came to Ufa, Salavat Yulaev had won the European hockey league, the Kontinental, for a second successive year. Any football team in the city risked being dwarfed by it.

There had been a couple of attempts to establish a football club in Ufa but both had folded. This was to be the third try. Building a club from scratch must be one of the most difficult tasks any manager can face.

If you come into an established club, you have a core of five or six players you can build a team round but we were just trying to get footballers from anywhere we could. We had a trial session for which about 150 hopefuls turned up and I had to select a squad from that. There was some money to offer them. The top wage I could pay would be 150,000 roubles a month (about £2,100).

It says something that two of those I picked, Pavel Alikin and Azmat Zaseyev, are still at Ufa, playing in the Russian Premier League. The vast majority of the team had never played together before. Our task was to win promotion to the Russian First Division – the second tier – in our first season.

We finished with 86 points, the same number as Neftekhimik, a club from a petrochemical town called Nizhnekamsk. They, however, had a better head-to-head record and were promoted. They are now a feeder club for Rubin Kazan.

Our stadium was the Neftyanik, a shallow open bowl that held 15,000, although the city's obsession with hockey meant it was never full. Even now in the Premier League it might get 12,000 for a game with Spartak Moscow; the average is about 3–4,000.

When I was managing Ufa in 2011, the stadium had artificial

grass that seemed to have been laid sometime in the 1950s. Three players broke their legs on it. The club was funded by the government of Bashkortostan. I decided to raise the problem of the pitch with them and suggested that, if Ufa did become a successful club, they might like to start looking for another stadium.

I was met with incredulity. The Neftyanik was perfect, I was told, because it was five minutes' walk from the government offices. There would be no question of looking for a new arena.

They did eventually accept that it might be better to play on real grass and I pointed out something else that had been troubling me since my arrival in Ufa. I had measured the pitch and one half was clearly bigger than the other.

Because Ufa was so dominated by ice hockey, it was hard to find even the most basic technical expertise when it came to football – and that included a decent groundsman. Despite finishing with 86 points, my contract with Ufa was not renewed.

Once we had been knocked out of the Russian Cup, which was the day he burst into the dressing room with a baseball bat, Gazizov, the club's sporting director, had wanted to sack me. We had lost on penalties. However, because Ufa was financed by the government of Bashkortostan, he wasn't able to do it. I told Gazizov I wanted him nowhere near my dressing room; but once the season was over, I had no enthusiasm for working with him again.

I was then appointed to be the assistant manager of FC Nizhny Novgorod, one of the great historic cities of the Russian empire built 250 miles east of Moscow, where the river Oka meets the Volga. I would be working under Gadzhi Gadzhiev, who had managed me at FC Saturn. It used to have two football teams but now it has none. Nizhny Novgorod were in the Russian Premier League when I arrived in 2012 but they couldn't pay their players. By 2016 the club had been liquidated.

My last club was Solyaris, a team in the third tier of Russian football, based in Moscow. I was appointed in January 2016 after their manager, Sergei Shustikov, died of a heart attack at the age of 45. They were third in their division when I took over and second when I was sacked three months later.

Only one team would be promoted into the Russian equivalent of the Championship, the National Football League, and even in January it was pretty clear it was not going to be Solyaris. I was told that, whatever the club's position in the table, the goal was still the same, promotion.

Even though we rose a place to second, Solyaris were still twelve points behind Khimki with seven games to go when the president, Vladimir Ovchinnikov, dismissed me.

The fact I had taken over a group of footballers with whom I was unfamiliar or that it might take time to promote Solyaris, whose ground had a capacity of just 5,000, did not occur to him.

When I was appointed, Ovchinnikov told me his ambition was to go to Monaco and watch Solyaris playing European football. He thought he could start planning his trip in three years.

After I'd stopped laughing, I realised that if I started relaying these instructions to the players, they would have thought me mad. However, the board was completely serious and when I asked the president and vice-president if they were joking I received only a series of deadpan stares.

It was quite a frightening experience to talk to people who truly believed this was possible. They imagined it could be done with sheer willpower alone. I told them the only way they were going to watch football in Monaco in three years' time was to pay at the gate.

14
MY HOME TOWN

ONE DAY, I CAME BACK TO THE PLACE WHERE I HAD
grown up, where I had learned about ice hockey, football and life.
I barely recognised Kirovograd.

The shops were full. When I was growing up, my mother would
buy what was available. If the shops only had potatoes, then we
ate potatoes. Now the supermarkets had plenty of food; there were
clothes to buy but there was also unemployment and on the streets
the signs of poverty were obvious. The food and clothes were available but only to those who could afford it. Supplies of gas and
electricity would be cut off; the pavements were crumbling. Suddenly, Kirovograd seemed to be a place where it wasn't advisable to
go out at night.

What was once the Soviet Union has changed out of all recognition. Has it changed for the better? Well, that depends for whom. There is an older generation that prefers the way things used to be. The younger generation, who did not live through Communism, cannot imagine how their grandparents put up with it.

Once, you might not have been able to get hold of a pair of jeans to go out in, but you could go out. You felt a sense of belonging. Some people might have earned a higher salary than you but there didn't seem to be the vast gulf between rich and poor that was now being flaunted on the streets of my home town.

It wasn't just happening in Kirovograd, it was a pattern spread across the old Soviet Union. I had seen it wherever I had gone to coach, repeated to a greater or lesser degree.

The smaller towns, places where there was perhaps one big factory that gave the place a purpose, suffered worse. The great cities did better.

My managerial career tended to be played out in the lower leagues in Russia. I would travel all over the country to medium-sized provincial towns and minor cities where you would come face to face with some terrible situations. There had been no progress whatsoever. The old industries, the steel works, the paper mills and the traditional factories, the places that provided so much work in the provinces, were dead or dying.

People were migrating to the cities to find work. For people from Ukraine, Kazakhstan, Tajikistan, it was Moscow that was the great draw. People told you that they had to get there because only there did work seem guaranteed and paid the kinds of salaries that would allow their families to live.

My life was changing fast. As my football career finished, so did my marriage. My wife Inna met Stas Mikhailov, who is Russia's most famous pop singer. I believe they met after one of his concerts in Moscow. I was shocked by what happened, stunned. I did not see it coming.

The divorce took a long time. Inna wanted the flat in Moscow, the house in Sussex for her and for the children. In Russia it was treated as a major scandal. Russia has gone for tabloid news in a very big way, as well as reality shows – which are usually a version of *Big Brother* or *Love Island*.

The pillars of the old Soviet newspaper industry have changed beyond recognition; *Izvestia* is now a tabloid. *Pravda*, where all the Communist Party's grand announcements used to be made, no longer comes out every day. You still won't find much news in it.

The most successful are papers whose news values are a cross between the *Sun* and the *Sunday Sport*. They wanted all the details of the breakdown of our marriage. I told them as little as I could.

In Italy the press was everywhere. *Gazzetta dello Sport* and *Corriere dello Sport* analysed your every touch of the ball. They had, however, no interest in your private life. Their only concern was how you trained and how you played.

Inna was interviewed on television to give her side of the divorce and I was offered a lot of money to do the same. I turned them down. A television studio is not the place to go through details of your marriage.

All I wanted was to be able to see the children again. Andrei would have been around sixteen and Eva eleven or twelve. They were hard times. I moved out of our flat in Moscow and found somewhere to rent. Perhaps that is why I accepted that job, working for Alisher Usmanov among the blast furnaces of Novotroitsk. It was very far away.

You cannot divorce a sportsman's private life from what you see in public. A spectator will always assume the person he is watching has no personal problems at all, that there is nothing on his mind but the game. Often, the spectator will be wrong.

There were many reasons why my second full season at Manchester United was not a success. Perhaps I was tired from the European Championship in Sweden. Perhaps defenders in England were getting used to my way of playing. Perhaps, too, the loss of our baby boy took its toll.

My relationship with my children is now back to what it was. They are both living in London. Andrei works for the Stellar Group agency advising them on football in eastern Europe while, as I write this, Eva is preparing to go to university to study politics and religion. They are good kids and I am very proud of them.

My mother still lives in Kirovograd and she travels to Israel to see my sister and her two girls, one of whom has just completed her national service in the Israeli army. That's my family and, like a lot of families, it is spread far and wide.

When the system collapsed, people's priorities changed. They had to find work; they had to find the money to keep their families going. They wondered what country they belonged to. Paying for football academies during all the foreign debt defaults suddenly seemed very low on the agenda.

After Euro 2012, the Russian Football Union signed a co-operation agreement with the German FA to try to tap into their expertise, particularly when it came to staging a World Cup. They fondly imagined that this alone would be enough.

When the German national team was in crisis after their dreadful performance in Euro 2000, they did not sign bits of paper. They overhauled their entire system of youth development; they brought in leading former players from all over Germany to help administer it. That they reached a World Cup final two years later did not deter them from following through with their reforms. They were not that easily satisfied.

We desperately need in Russia the kind of football academies that used to exist across the whole Soviet Union, administered by people who have some connection with the game. The Soviet Union existed for around seventy years and in that time it formed a way of doing things, a tradition that was swept away along with everything else.

When my generation, the last of the Soviet footballers who learned their trade in the old system, finished there was very little to replace them.

When I was playing for Manchester United there were about fifteen footballers from the old country plying their trade in what we used to call the West – in Spain, England, France and Germany. That export stream has dried up completely.

We need to rediscover that drive to find young footballers that used to be such a feature of the Soviet Union. Russian football has academies now but they are ones you have to pay to go to. When I was growing up in Kirovograd, they were interested in your ability as a footballer, not your parents' ability to pay.

When I was managing Torpedo Zil, we had an academy right next to the training ground and one day two cars pulled up. The first was a security car. These were serious visitors. From the second car, a ten-year-old boy emerged dressed in an immaculate full Barcelona kit, wearing gleaming boots.

The kit was the only thing about him that suggested he might make a professional. The boy was, shall we say, rather podgy. He possessed no football ability whatsoever, although he did bring two bodyguards with him.

There was nothing the club could have done for the boy except to advise him to steer clear of McDonald's. Other clubs might have taken him on just on the basis of what his parents might pay.

I was born in 1969 but imagine if I had been born 35 years later. When I was a teenager I lived for football, but my dad died when I was seventeen. My mother was a single parent; she couldn't have afforded the fees. Where would a poor boy like me, burning to prove himself, go? There would have been several paths in front of me but one would have led towards organised crime.

The biggest problem Russian football has is that it is too often run by men who do not understand the game. The big Russian clubs, like CSKA Moscow and Zenit St Petersburg, tend to be well run. Spartak, once the Soviet Union's most successful club, has its own stadium for the first time in its history and there are some smaller clubs, like Krasnodar, who have good presidents. However, far too many are footballing banana republics.

Typically, the club president will have a team of 'advisors' surrounding him. They are his paid courtiers whose jobs depend on telling the president precisely what he wants to hear.

So if the president declares in a board meeting, 'I think we should be in the Champions League within three seasons,' instead of pointing out the impracticalities of this proposal, the advisors will simply nod their heads. Maybe one will try to impress the president by suggesting they can win the Champions League in four years. Then they will put enormous pressure on the manager to make sure these wishes are fulfilled. When they are not – because they cannot be fulfilled – the manager finds himself unemployed.

Anzhi Makhachkala was a club like that. Its president was Suleyman Kerimov, a financial wizard who grew up in Dagestan, in southern Russia by the Caspian Sea. He threw grand parties and flew over the likes of Amy Winehouse to sing at them. He was nearly killed when he crashed his Ferrari on the Promenade des Anglais in Nice.

Makhachkala was like Belfast in the 1970s. There were shootings, bombs and atrocities, but Kerimov became interested in football and in turning his home town into one of the centres of the European game.

Kerimov brought in Roberto Carlos, Yuri Zhirkov from Chelsea and Samuel Eto'o from Inter Milan and paid them huge sums of money. Eto'o was said to be earning more than £16m a year. For Roberto Carlos's birthday, Kerimov gave him a Bugatti Veyron and when Eto'o said he wanted to watch a game in Italy, he laid on his own private jet. He hired Guus Hiddink to coach them.

Because of the terrorism in Dagestan, the players lived and trained in Moscow and only flew down to Makhachkala on the day of the game. When they qualified for the Europa League, they played their home fixtures at the Luzhniki in Moscow.

Anzhi did well under Hiddink. In the Europa League group matches, they won their three home games against Liverpool, Young Boys Bern and Udinese and made it to the round of sixteen, where they lost narrowly to Newcastle.

Hiddink took them to third place in the Russian Premier League, behind CSKA and Zenit. It was a superb achievement but it was not enough to qualify Anzhi for the Champions League.

Hiddink resigned in the summer of 2013 and was replaced by Rene Meulensteen, who had been Manchester United's first-team coach under Sir Alex Ferguson. Meulensteen lasted sixteen days before he was sacked.

Then one day the money stopped. Kerimov had lost interest. The stars left and Anzhi were relegated in last place. Kerimov sold the club in 2016 and it is owned by a businessman called Osman Kadiev, who might not have Kerimov's money but who might give Anzhi something as valuable – stability.

Other aspects of football were changing. I spent most of my career as a winger, the kind of positon that Ferguson and Valery Lobanovsky loved and a position that long ago disappeared. The old 4–4–2 system that inspired Dynamo Kiev and Manchester United has been almost completely discarded.

I played my best football in that system with Manchester United. When I look back on my career, there was never a club where everything went smoothly. There were always hiccups, always moments of doubt.

If you look at my medals, you would have to say my time at Old Trafford saw me at my peak, between the ages of 22 and 26. I won the Treble in my first season at Glasgow Rangers but the standard of football in Scotland was lower than the Premier League or Serie A. I enjoyed the trophies but that knowledge rather tempered the triumph. I didn't win a trophy in my eighteen months at Everton but I probably enjoyed my football at Goodison Park more than anywhere else.

If I imagine myself as the teenager travelling on the bus to Nikolai Koltsov's academy in Kharkov, I would have smiled if I had been told what I might achieve in the game. But, even so, looking back now I could and should have done better. There are some decisions I took that I would change. I should not have left Manchester United in 1995. Had I had an advisor or someone in the team I could really have trusted who could have told me: 'No, Andrei, this can be sorted without you leaving the club,' I probably would have stayed. The person on whom I leaned for advice, Grigori Essaoulenko, had a very firm financial interest in getting me out of Old Trafford.

I am still in contact with some of my former managers: with Sir Alex Ferguson, with Claudio Ranieri and with Alberto Malesani. Despite all our difficulties at Ibrox, when Dick Advocaat became manager of Zenit St Petersburg I was able to have a conversation with him. There is no point in revisiting old battlefields and reprising old rows. The wounds have healed.

Had the Soviet Union not broken apart, my international career might have been very different. It was a nation of fifteen republics. On a long winter night you can pretend to put them back together and try to pick a team that would have graced World Cups or European Championships. You can do the same for Yugoslavia.

I have a picture of myself winning the European Under-21 title with the Soviet Union in 1990 on the night we beat Yugoslavia. The two teams were crammed full of talent and they had more of a future than the countries whose shirts they wore. Even Simferopol in the Crimea, where we won the trophy, was to have a very interesting history. Its citizens would be first Soviet, then Ukrainian and then Russian without ever leaving their homes.

It mirrored my own career. Although I could have made more of it, I am proud of my time as a footballer. I played for two of the greatest managers in world football and was part of a great Manchester United side. The experiences of Glasgow, Merseyside and Serie A will stay with me always. I was the last Soviet footballer, or at least the last footballer who scored a goal for the Soviet Union. The last in a very fine line.

SOVIET FOOTBALL – AN EDUCATION
SERGEI BALTACHA

SERGEI BALTACHA PLAYED FOR DYNAMO KIEV between 1976 and 1989 and was capped 45 times by the Soviet Union. He is under-17 and under-18 manager at Charlton Athletic.

I remember meeting Nick Faldo just after he had won more than $1m in a golf tournament. After our conversation, Faldo told me he was going off to practise. 'I am off to do my ten thousand hours,' he said.

To most people, it would seem odd that what Faldo really wanted to do immediately after a triumph was to practise some more drives. However, I understood exactly what he meant and so would Andrei Kanchelskis.

Ten thousand hours is a concept that, if you want to be a great pianist or a tennis player or a footballer, the only sure path to making it is through repetition and practice.

It wasn't called ten thousand hours when Andrei and I attended Nikolai Koltsov's academy in Kharkov but the key to our success was the constant practice he insisted on.

Andrei and I were a generation apart. I am eleven years older and when he came to Dynamo Kiev I was given the task of looking after him.

Our football education was the same. Perhaps because of Valery Lobanovsky's influence at Dynamo Kiev, the Ukraine had much more of a reputation for developing footballers for the Soviet Union than Russia did.

Even though Nikolai Koltsov died in 2011 and his academy has long closed, that reputation has continued. Dynamo Kiev's budget for their academy is $125,000 a year and they regularly produce footballers that graduate to the Champions League. The budget for Charlton's academy is £1.5m, which is a fraction of what clubs like Chelsea and Manchester City spend on theirs – and you have to ask how many Premier League footballers do they produce?

In the squad that we took to the 1982 World Cup twelve players were from Ukraine. When we reached the final of the 1988 European Championship in West Germany, Lobanovsky's squad had thirteen from Ukraine.

More specifically, when we went to Tunisia to win the Under-20 World Cup in 1977, five of that side were graduates of the Kharkov academy. Three years later we won the European Under-21 championship.

The Kharkov academy recruited the best players from across the Ukraine. I grew up in Mariupol where the Donbass mining region meets the Sea of Azov.

I had been voted the best centre forward in my region and, as result, I was sent to Koltsov's academy at the age of fourteen.

It was like a boarding school. You went home every four months. A typical day would begin at seven o'clock. You had an hour to prepare for the session, unsupervised. You might practise keeping the ball up or you might go for a jog. After the training session there would be two hours of school. Then lunch, then a two-hour session, then homework and then sleep.

Koltsov had been one of the very best central defenders of his era and had played alongside Lobanovsky when Dynamo Kiev won the Soviet championship in 1961.

You might have thought him a very hard man but to me he was not hard, he was interested in giving you a reality check. If you are doing well at fourteen, it means nothing. His only interest was whether you signed a professional contract at nineteen.

More than forty years after I first met him, I am still using some of Koltsov's techniques at the Charlton academy. Like Lobanovsky, he never shouted or was aggressive to you. Koltsov would not call you 'Sergei' or 'Andrei' but 'Dear Sergei' or 'Dear Andrei'.

Playing for Dynamo Kiev, you knew Lobanovsky was disappointed with you when he came into the dressing room laughing to himself.

From the moment I started coaching in Britain I could not believe how the parents of young footballers would stand on the touchline and abuse not just their kids but other young players and the referee without having any real knowledge of the game themselves.

When they questioned why I was telling them to shut up, I told them I had been voted the best footballer in a country of 250m people and I had some idea of what I was talking about.

I went to England two years before Andrei. It was very different. Andrei was at the start of his career; I was coming to the end of mine.

I'd been signed by Ipswich. Their manager was John Duncan. On my debut we were playing Stoke at Portman Road. I was played out of position on the right wing and got a sore neck from looking up as the ball was continually launched high into the air.

At half time, Duncan burst into the dressing room, threw a cup of tea against the wall and shouted: 'Fuck, fuck, fuck'. Like Andrei, I had George Scanlan as my interpreter and he was sitting next to me. I asked George what Duncan had said and he replied: 'He is talking about sex'. We won that game 5-1.

To someone like Nikolai Koltsov or Valery Lobanovsky, shouting like this would have seemed pointless. What information are you trying to give by screaming at people?

I never quite understood that and something else I don't understand is when a player misses from five yards the coach shouts: 'Unlucky'.

It's not unlucky. It's not good enough. Koltsov would never have used those words. He would have told the player to make sure he used a better technique. If you missed an easy volley in tennis, your coach would not say you were unlucky.

It was a strict regime and it was the same when you graduated to play for Dynamo Kiev. You would be given regular blood tests and physical and psychological tests every month and this was in the 1970s. The blood tests and weighing were done every morning. Lobanovsky was thirty years ahead of his time.

Frankly, I was disappointed with the standard of British football I encountered. I thought it would have been more professional.

Shortly after I arrived in Ipswich I was told that Bobby Robson wanted to see me. He was then England manager and still lived not far from the town.

I had been part of the Soviet Union side that had beaten England in a friendly at Wembley in 1984 and then four years later we had overcome them 3-1 in Frankfurt in the European Championships.

Bobby came to my house, where I met him with George Scanlan. We talked for two or three hours about how the Soviet Union produced young footballers but Robson's first question was: 'Sergei, why do you keep beating us?' We had done our ten thousand hours and they had not – and I still don't think they do.

We had a different mentality then. The authorities set great store by education. I had a law degree. When Germany won the World Cup in 2014, Joachim Low pointed out that many of his footballers were academically intelligent.

For Andrei, it would have been hard going from this scientific approach to football to an English dressing room in the 1990s, especially one run by Alex Ferguson.

The first time I came across Ferguson was in 1990 when I was playing in Willie Miller's testimonial in Aberdeen. He was managing the Rest of the World team. We had never met before but he knew so much about me and I was amazed he had taken the trouble to find out. He was so charming and he asked about my son, who was showing a lot of promise, and invited him for a trial at Manchester United.

There was also another side to Alex Ferguson. When I was assistant manager of St Mirren I worked for Tony Fitzpatrick, who had been captain of St Mirren when Ferguson managed the club.

He told me that they were playing Celtic and before the game

Ferguson had told his defenders to pick up the number nine and in the first minute the striker scored in precisely the way Ferguson predicted he would.

When Ferguson came into the dressing room, he picked up a metal urn that usually contained hot water for tea and hurled it at the defenders who had forgotten his instructions almost as soon as he had issued them. It hit the wall near to where Tony was sitting.

That sort of behaviour would never have been tolerated in the Soviet Union. Not only did Andrei go to a club in a league where he had never played before and to a country whose language he did not understand, he was managed by a man who could be full of charm and knowledge one day and then lose his temper like that on another. It would have been hard for him to know what make of it all.

Andrei was a strong-willed character and he got into a lot of arguments but many of them, I am sure, resulted from the jump in mentality you had to take when moving from the Soviet Union to a British football dressing room in 1991.

Manchester United was, however, the making of Andrei Kanchelskis. He did not play a lot for Dynamo Kiev. His style was an English style and he needed to find a team that suited him. That team was Alex Ferguson's Manchester United.

When he first started playing for Manchester United, I remember thinking 'Oh my God, this is astonishing'. In Kiev we didn't use our midfield to get behind the defence as Andrei used his power and speed to do at Old Trafford.

They had a 4-4-2 system that Andrei really enjoyed, especially when you had Ryan Giggs on the other flank, and it enabled him to exploit one of English football's biggest weaknesses – their central defenders, who tended to be very slow. The combination of Kanchelskis and Giggs on either flank would have been terrifying for any defender.

He was not so successful in Italy when he went to play for Fiorentina but Serie A did not suit him. There was not the space behind the back four to give him the freedom he so enjoyed.

However, in England at his peak, he could be astonishing. Between 1992-1996 he was one of the best players in England and sometimes with Manchester United he could claim to be the best of all. Whenever I watched him it was with a surge of pride – not just for what he had achieved but because of where he had come from.

AFTERWORD
JOE ROYLE

ONE OF THE GAMES OF ANDREI KANCHELSKIS'S
life was the FA Cup semi-final for Manchester United against my
Oldham side. We had got very near to reaching a first FA Cup final
in the club's history in the first game at Wembley, but in the replay
Andrei's performance was astonishing.

I'd been interested in him long before that night at Maine
Road. I'd followed his progress ever since he arrived in England. I'd
watched his first game for Manchester United reserves.

When I watched him it wasn't with the thought that I might
one day manage him. Oldham could never have afforded Andrei
Kanchelskis.

However, Everton were a different club and when he didn't play
for Manchester United against us in the 1995 FA Cup final and

stories about his deteriorating relationship with Alex Ferguson began to appear in the press, I did wonder.

I was on holiday in Tenerife when his interpreter, George Scanlan, phoned me and said: 'Joe, I don't know if you're aware of it but Andrei's probably going to Middlesbrough.' I came home immediately to try to sort out a deal to bring him to Goodison Park.

Although I was aware that the presence of Bryan Robson made Middlesbrough an attractive option for Andrei, I thought Everton would suit him more.

We were on a strong upward curve. Everton had been bottom of the Premier League when I arrived but we'd gone on to win the FA Cup and the Charity Shield.

The players were there and the prospect of bringing a marquee signing to Goodison made me think we could take Everton to another level. In the summer of 1995 Andrei was exactly what I was looking for. I had seen close up what he could do and his coming would whet the appetite of the fans.

I went to his home to persuade him to join Everton. I tried to talk him out of going to Middlesbrough by joking that he would be going back to Chernobyl, although I am not sure he saw the humour in that.

Andrei was easy to manage. At the start of the transfer there was all sorts of stuff coming out of the United end saying he was a gambler or that he was involved with the Russian mafia, which turned out to be so much nonsense.

From the moment he came to the club to sign for us, he was a total professional. He had a deep desire to win and the lads in the dressing room loved him. So did the supporters, to the extent that fans who had been going to Goodison long before Andrei's arrival regularly name him in their all-time best Everton XIs.

His first season may have been magnificent for us but he didn't start it well. There was a long delay while Shakhtar Donetsk haggled over how much of the transfer fee they were entitled to and he was injured almost as soon as he started playing. However, by the end of the season he had sixteen goals in 32 games. Not one of those goals was a penalty or a free-kick.

I never thought of Andrei as a winger. To me, he was always a wide striker. There were crosses that Duncan Ferguson scored from, but Andrei created as many chances by hitting the ball so hard that the keeper couldn't hold the shot and Duncan or someone else would devour the rebound.

The other way Andrei created goals was by creating space. He was so strong and powerful going forward that the opposition defenders would back off him.

He had a great rapport with Anders Limpar, who could not believe we had signed him. When I first came to Everton, Anders asked me for a transfer. His agent had set up a deal for him to go to Japan. He said he wanted to leave because there was a lot of hostility at Goodison towards him because he had given away the penalty in the game against Wimbledon that Everton had to win to stay in the Premier League.

I told Anders I rated him and had admired how he'd played at Arsenal, and he responded with some inspired performances in the rest of that season. At the end of that campaign I told him he would be playing on the other flank to Andrei Kanchelskis. He found that a mouth-watering prospect.

We had a great coach in Willie Donachie, a totally dedicated pro who maintained the same weight and fitness levels he had when he was a player. The fans were behind us and, with Andrei, we had a very good team. In the summer of 1996 , after his superb first season for the club, Everton were being talked about as championship contenders.

His best game, of course was the derby at Anfield in which he scored twice. One ex-Liverpool player, who was working as a radio commentator on the day, made a fool of himself by declaring that Everton had won 'through long-ball football'.

That was nonsense. The move than involved Anders and Paul Rideout and which finished with Andrei heading into the net was a very long way from long-ball football. The other goal was a shot that was simply too strong for David James to save. That is the goal that epitomised how I saw him; as a powerful, wide striker.

Andrei, it was true, did not tackle much but that didn't really bother me. I hadn't bought him to tackle – I'd bought Earl Barrett to do that. At right-back Earl could handle two people coming at him. Andrei's instructions were quite simple: 'Make sure you are looking at their full-back when they get the ball. You can stand as far as you want away from him but I don't want to see you chasing the full-back.'

His second season was not as successful as his first. I didn't know his personal details but I got the sense that things were closing in on him. His son, Andrei, was poorly, he was being troubled by an ankle injury and he was being put under constant pressure from agents in Italy because they knew that clubs in Serie A wanted to sign him. There was a part of him that wanted a change and he thought abroad was the place where he could find it.

At the same time Everton were stuttering. We were being weighed down by injuries, the Liverpool Echo had turned against me, despite the fact that this had been my first poor spell since coming to the club, and Andrei's form was starting to suffer.

We had been knocked out of the League Cup at York and then we were knocked out of the FA Cup at home to Bradford. Andrei had been awful; he had meandered across the pitch, lost the ball and allowed Chris Waddle to score with a forty-yard chip.

There were a lot of little things going wrong and it seemed to get on top of him. When Fiorentina made their bid it would, to Andrei, have come at precisely the right time.

Looking back, what I should have done was to say to Andrei: 'Go away for a month, have a break and sort your injury out. Go abroad, get some sun and then come back to us.'

Perhaps I should have been stronger about it. Perhaps I should have bent a little bit earlier. His time with Everton was much too short.

I am still in touch with Andrei and his family and when he comes back to Merseyside for dinners or signings he gets a great reception because in the very real sense of the word Andrei Kanchelskis was a star.

ANDREI KANCHELSKIS' CAREER NOTES

DYNAMO KIEV

1989/90

Soviet Top League - Apps: 22. Goals: 1

In his first full season as a professional Andrei helped Dynamo Kiev to their 13th league title, helping the Ukrainians leap above Spartak Moscow as the most successful football club in the history of the Soviet Union. From his position on the wing, Andrei was providing the service for Oleg Protesov, the legendary striker who would join Olympiacos of Greece at the end of the campaign. Dynamo would beat CSKA Moscow to the championship, with manager Valery Lobanovsky blooding several young players alongside Andrei. Viktor Onopko, Yuri Nikiforov, Oleg Luzhny, Oleg Salenko and Sergey Yuran would all play in different European countries in the 1990s.

SHAKHTAR DONETSK

1990/91

Soviet Top League - Apps: 21. Goals: 3

Though it proved to be a significant season in Andrei's career: the last in his homeland for 13 years, Shakhtar Donetsk finished a disappointing 12th position in the final edition of Soviet Top League before the collapse of the Union. Andrei would ultimately be one of many Soviet players to leave the country in the same summer. While forward Igor Korneev was one of three CSKA Moscow players to join Spain's Espanyol, Spartak Moscow's midfielder Igor Shalimov would sign for Foggia and he would remain in Italy's Serie A for the next nine years. The great Alexandr Mostovoi, meanwhile, would leave for Portugal's Benfica.

MANCHESTER UNITED

1990/91

First Division - Apps: 1. Goals: 0.

Andrei signed for Manchester United at the end of March, making his debut in the penultimate game of the season in a 3-0 defeat to Crystal Palace. Manager Alex Ferguson decided to field a weakened side at Selhurst Park, with United facing Barcelona in the European Cup Winners' Cup final the next week. Andrei had not been signed in time to play in that game, but was present in Rotterdam as his new team won 2-1. Many consider this result as the one that injected United with the confidence to dominate English football over the next decade.

1991/92

First Division – Apps: 34. Goals: 5

Andrei settled down quickly in his first full season at Old Trafford, with Alex Ferguson preferring to play with two wingers like his former manager at Dynamo Kiev, Valery Lobanovskiy. Andrei scored his first goal against and Sheffield United, and gained his first silverware with a Super Cup victory over Red Star Belgrade. United soon followed that success with a League Cup triumph over Nottingham Forest. However, United could not keep pace with Leeds United in the league, slipping against Luton, Forest, West Ham and Liverpool at the end of the campaign, results which handed the title to their Yorkshire rivals.

1992/93

Premier League – Apps: 27. Goals: 3

A year that ended with United as the first champions of the newly rebranded Premier League, though one without Andrei in the side. The campaign had not started well for United and having taken just one point from the opening three league games, Andrei was dropped from the team in favour of Lee Sharpe. As the season progressed Andrei was increasingly used from the start in away fixtures, with Alex Ferguson appreciating his pace would allow United to punish opponents on the counter attack. It culminated with United's first league title since 1967.

1993/94

Premier League - 31. Goals: 7

Andrei's best season in English football to date, one which albeit began Ferguson persuading him to stay at United after he'd asked to leave following the frustrations of the previous year. Though he was sent-off during the 3-1 League Cup final defeat to Aston Villa, Andrei would play a decisive role in the 4-1 FA Cup semi-final replay against Oldham, later starting in the 4-0 rout of Chelsea in the final at Wembley just a week after signing a new five-year deal. United were the dominant force in the league, amassing 92 points and that meant another title was added to the record books.

1994/95

Premier League - Apps: 30. Goals: 14

If 1993/94 was the year in which Andrei started to make a major impact at Old Trafford, 1994/95 was truly the season in which he truly came alive. The winger scored 14 league goals in 30 appearances and eleven of them had come before the start of the new year. This spree included a two goals against champions to be Blackburn, and a hat-trick against rivals Manchester City. However, United, hamstrung by the suspension of Eric Cantona after *that* Crystal Palace incident, failed to overtake Blackburn on the final day after drawing with West Ham. By this stage Andrei was injured, and the failure of the United doctor to diagnose a double hernia would lead to a breakdown in relations. Although the club wanted him to stay, a £5 million move to Everton eventually seemed to suit all parties.

EVERTON

1995/96

Premier League - Apps 32 Goals: 16

Andrei's absence through injury had helped Everton beat Manchester United in the 1995 FA Cup final, and now Joe Royle turned to his new signing to give his *Dogs of War* midfield an extra dimension. Delays in negotiations meant Andrei frustratingly missed out on the narrow defeat to Feyenoord in the European Cup Winners' Cup, but he made up for lost time by scoring twice at Anfield on his debut, helping his side to a famous derby win. He would maintain good scoring form all season, and the duel threat he posed with Sweden's Anders Limpar helped Everton challenge for a European spot. His hat-trick in the penultimate fixture at Hillsborough helped keep this dream alive, but the Toffees would narrowly miss out on the last day to Arsenal.

1996/97

Premier League – Apps: 20. Goals: 4

Despite a resoundingly successful first season at Goodison Park, Andrei approached the 1996/97 campaign having appeared in Russia's disappointing Euro 96 campaign, a tournament held in England. Though he twice in the early 7-1 drubbing of Southampton, six straight defeats between Boxing Day and the end of January resulted in Joe Royle's sacking. It was in the middle of this run that Andrei was summoned to a meeting with the Everton directors, where they revealed an agreement to sell him to Fiorentina for £8 million. Within hours he was on a flight to sign for the Italian club.

FIORENTINA

1996/97

Serie A – Apps: 9. Goals: 0

Andrei had found the transition from Manchester to Liverpool an easy one to make, but moving to Florence was a far more difficult step. It took him six months to learn the language, and at the same time he had to get used to a new style of football Italy, with a heavier emphasis on defence, more possession and less counter-attacking. Andrei featured nine times in the league, but did not get on the scoresheet. His new boss Claudio Ranieri was sacked at the end of the campaign as Fiorentina finished ninth in Serie A.

1997/98

Serie A – Apps: 17 Goals: 2

Andrei scored in the second game of the season during a 3-1 win over Bari, and then on the last day in a 2-0 victory over AC Milan, but he admits everything in between proved to be a rather forgettable experience. He picked up an ankle injury in the third game of the campaign against Inter Milan, and on his return to the fold he broke his kneecap in the first leg of Russia's World Cup qualifying play-off, ironically against Italy. In total he made 17 appearances in the league for Fiorentina that campaign, as the team finished fifth under Alberto Malesani. Andrei had played his last game for the *Viola*.

GLASGOW RANGERS

1998/99

Scottish Premier League – Apps: 31. Goals: 7

Glasgow was Andrei's next destination, with ambitious chairman David Murray willing to sanction a £5.5 million move. This was the age of Rangers dominance in Scotland, though it was a difficult start for Andrei on a personal level. In his first Old Firm derby he broke his arm and in the second, Celtic hammered Rangers, 5-1. Nevertheless, Rangers would proceed to win the treble under Dick Advocaat that season, sealing the title at Celtic Park and beating their fierce rivals in the Scottish Cup Final.

1999/2000

Scottish Premier League – Apps: 28 Goals: 4

Andrei enjoyed more success during his second season at Ibrox. A regular fixture in the starting line-up, Rangers cruised to the title by a huge 21 points. Having scored twice in a 5-1 victory over Motherwell, Andrei then scored his first Old Firm goal in a 4-0 win. In Europe Rangers disappointed, however: failing to make it out of a difficult Champions League group containing PSV Eindhoven, Valencia and Bayern Munich. Though Rangers would clinch the Scottish Cup with a 4-0 win over Aberdeen, Andrei's relationship with Dick Advocaat was beginning to disintegrate.

2000/2001

Scottish Premier League – Apps: 7. Goals: 1

This was the season in Scotland in which Rangers' dominance started to wane, with Martin O'Neill reviving Celtic. Andrei was having a tough time of it: of the seven league appearances he made, four were from the bench, and of the seven Champions League matches he featured in, five were as a substitute. Rangers could not make it past a Champions League group containing Sturm Graz, Monaco and Galatasaray, and once again fell short in the UEFA Cup, losing over two legs to Kaiserslautern. After a training ground bust up with Fernando Ricksen, the Dutch defender, Andrei was soon on the move again.

MANCHESTER CITY

2000/2001

Premier League – Apps: 10. Goals: 0

Out of the Rangers team, Andrei sought first team football. It was Joe Royle, his former manager at Everton, who showed an interest, and so Andrei spent the rest of the season at Manchester City on loan, joining the club at a difficult time, with City three points from safety with 14 games left. Though Andrei scored against old rivals Liverpool at Anfield in the FA Cup his arrival did not alter the league pattern and City would be relegated, along with Coventry City and Bradford City.

GLASGOW RANGERS

2001/2002

Scottish Premier League – Apps: 10. Goals: 1

After Manchester City's relegation, Andrei turned to his parent club Rangers where his relationship with Dick Advocaat went unrepaired. When Hibernian boss Alex McLeish succeeded Advocaat, Andrei was told that his Rangers career was over. His only goal that season – where Rangers finished second to Celtic – was against Kilmarnock during a 5-0 victory.

SOUTHAMPTON

2002/2003

Premier League – Apps: 1. Goals: 0

A free agent for the first time in his professional career, Andrei now had to find a new club. After training with Gordon Strachan at Southampton, he signed a short-term contract on the south coast but the move did not go well. Andrei made one substitute appearance in the Premier League against Sheffield Wednesday, and one substitute appearance in the League Cup during a 6-1 win over Tranmere. His time in England was almost up.

AL-HILAL

2003

Saudi Professional League - Apps: 3. Goals: 0

Al-Hilal, the most successful club in Saudi Arabian history with 15 league titles, were in the middle of a transitional period when Andrei arrived at the club, a period which did not see them end the season as champions for three years. While Al-Hilal, from the capital Riyadh, would finish the 2002/03 campaign in fifth position, some eight points off the pace at the summit of the table, Jeddah's Al-Itihad would emerge as champions.

SATURN MOSCOW

2005

Russian Premier League - Apps: 39. Goals: 4

Suddenly, the Russian Premier League was now sufficiently awash with the level of ambition to encourage a big influx of foreigners and returning natives. Russian captain and long-time Spanish exile Viktor Onopko, for example, spurned Everton in favour of a move to Russian mid-table outfit Saturn and eventually, Andrei would join him after a move to Dinamo Moscow did not happen. It would prove to be a season where Saturn would finish in eleventh place, some way behind the biggest Moscow clubs led by CSKA, Spartak and Lokomotiv.

KRYLIA SOVETOV

2006

Russian Premier League - Apps: 21. Goals 1

It was Andrei's last season as a professional footballer, though he did not expect it to be. "I have enough desire and energy to continue," he said after Krylia finished ninth. "I played 22 games, I feel no tiredness at all and I think I did well. I'm sure I'll find a new team very soon. I have a couple of offers from abroad but, to be honest, I would prefer to play in a Russian club." And yet, Andrei eventually decided to retire. "You need to leave at the right time," he later concluded. "Now seems a suitable moment to begin a new chapter in my footballing life."

TORPEDO-ZIL MOSCOW

2010

Russian Second Division

Following two seasons as the general director at FC Nosta Novotroitsk, Andrei returned to Moscow to start his first job in management. Torpedo-Zil Moscow was a club founded by workers at a newspaper and a nearby car plant less than a decade earlier, rising from the regional championships to the third tier of Russian football, which geographically is divided into five zones due to the enormous size of the country. Torpedo-Zil narrowly missed out on promotion to the first division under Andrei, finishing four points behind champions Torpedo Vladimir.

FC UFA

2011

Russian Second Division

By 2017, FC Ufa had risen to become a competitive Russian Premier League club but back in 2011, it had just formed and Andrei was appointed as their first manager. Like at Torpedo-Zil, Ufa performed well and finished their debut season joint top of the table with Neftekhimik Nizhnekamsk. Ufa's poorer head-to-head record saw Neftekhimik win the title. However, Dynamo Bryansk's failure to meet licensing requirements for the 2012/13 Russian First Division and this resulted in Ufa receiving an unexpected promotion.

JURMALA

2014

Latvian Higher League

Jurmala were already as good as relegated from Latvia's top flight by the time Andrei was appointed to his third managerial position at a club that had only formed six years before. Jurmala had suffered from economic problems and point deductions, contributing towards a last placed finish in the ten team league, which was eventually won by Ventspils at a canter. Andrei had arrived in Latvia following a period as Volga's assistant manager in the Russian Premier League.

SOLYARIS MOSCOW

2016

Russian Second Division

Another club with limited history but high ambition, Solyaris were formed only in 2014 and under Andrei were in line to finish second in the third tier of Russian football, albeit 12 points behind champions, Khimki. With seven matches remaining, considering only the division's winners were promoted at the end of the season, Andrei was fired from his positon. Had he seen out the rest of the campaign, he probably would have led a team to a second place finish at this level of Russian football for the third time in his career.

ACKNOWLEDGEMENTS

MANY THANKS TO THE PEOPLE INVOLVED IN THE production of this book: Ian Allen, Jonathan Burd, Veronica Miller, Galina Hutchinson, Nathalie Altukhova, Phil Dickinson, Dave Cockram, Thomas Regan; plus Sergei Baltacha, Joe Royle, Ryan Giggs, Sam Wallace, my son Andrei Jr and my daughter Eva.

INDEX

Olympic (Luzhniki) Stadium 1, 3, 9, 65, 189, 203

Otkrytie Stadium 3–4, 34

Moshiri, Farhad 119

Mostovoi, Aleksandar 42

Mourinho, Jose 51, 77, 103

Moyes, David 93, 103, 112

Murray, David 140–1, 145, 152, 158, 170

player signings 148–9, 157, 162

Nagorno-Karabakh 31

Naples 126, 127–8

Napoli (football team) 127

Neftekhimik 193

Neville, Gary 101, 113, 186

Newcastle United 115, 168

Nizhny Novgorod 194–5

Nosta Novotroitsk 186, 187–8

Novotroitsk 186–8, 199

Numan, Arthur 149, 151, 157

Oborin, Sergei 185, 186

Old Trafford

AK first game at 58

AK last game at 169

Olympic Games (1980) 1

O'Neill, Martin 152, 161, 169

Ovchinnnikov, Vladimir 195

Ovett, Steve 1

Pagliuca, Gianluca 135

Paisley, Bob 48

Palchikov, Sergei 42

Pallister, Gary 61, 77

PAOK Salonika 158

Parker, Paul 77, 95

Parma 131, 137, 139–40, 158–9

Pavlyuchenko, Roman 53

penalties 160–1

Petrovsky, Valentin 30

Pirlo, Andrea 156

Poborsky, Karol 101

Pogrebnyak, Pavel 150

Porrini, Sergio 159

Premier League, Serie A vs 133–4

Prodan, Daniel 149

PSV Eindhoven 149, 151, 157, 158, 159, 160

Putin, Vladimir 2, 150

Ramenskoye 181

Ramsden, Ken 97

Ranger see Glasgow Rangers

Ranieri, Claudio 124, 132–3, 134, 205

Reagan, Ronald 2

Rebrov, Sergei 31, 102, 177

Red Star Belgrade 58, 59

Repka, Tomas 136

Ricksen, Fernando 149, 150, 151, 163

Rideout, Paul 113

Riyadh 171, 173, 175–6

Deera Square 175–6

Robson, Bobby 50, 133

Robson, Bryan 53, 64, 74, 83, 129

card-playing 174

as manager 93, 108–9

Rodionov, Vladimir 42

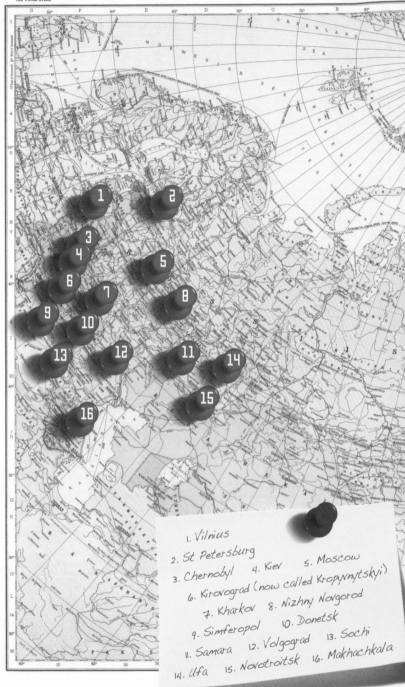

1. Vilnius
2. St Petersburg
3. Chernobyl   4. Kiev   5. Moscow
6. Kirovograd (now called Kropyvnytskyi)
7. Kharkov   8. Nizhny Novgorod
9. Simferopol   10. Donetsk
11. Samara   12. Volgograd   13. Sochi
14. Ufa   15. Novotroitsk   16. Makhachkala